Killing the Church

The Failure to Confront

DR. JEFF PARKER

T0105508

Previously Published Works

Kidnapped for Christmas

Killing the Church

Dr. Jeff Parker

WestBow
PRESS
A DIVISION OF THOMAS NELSON

WestBow Press books may be ordered through booksellers or by contacting:

WestBow Press
A Division of Thomas Nelson
1663 Liberty Drive
Bloomington, IN 47403
www.westbowpress.com
1-(866) 928-1240

ISBN: 978-1-4497-5728-1 (e)
ISBN: 978-1-4497-5729-8 (sc)
ISBN: 978-1-4497-5730-4 (hc)

Library of Congress Control Number: 2012911157

Printed in the United States of America

WestBow Press rev. date: 8/24/2012

DEDICATION

For Jesus Christ and my wife, children, and church

The failure to confront is killing your church,
your marriage, and every relationship you hold dear.
—

CONTENTS

PREFACE

There are times in a man's life when God puts upon his heart the impossible, a call to attempt a task that is beyond him. This work has been such an undertaking. I would have preferred to say that this has been a pleasant experience, one filled with the warmness that no doubt comes to those who spend their lives tucked behind paper, writing thoughts that will in time occupy the minds of their readers. However, what I have written has been pushed and prodded by a divine unction, a drive, an abandonment—one in which the Enemy has constantly peered over my shoulder, bringing an endless barrage of conflict, haunting every letter. For it is most assured that Satan delights in a dirty bride, a church that has grown lax, abandoning her call to holiness. Unkempt and mismanaged, her members meander in and out of the disciplines of the faith with little if any accountability. She no longer greets with a "Maranatha" but rather hunkers down in the contaminant from which she has been called to change. So in regard to our enemy, he is most assuredly distressed over the pages you are about to read. Why? Perhaps another reformation of sorts is on the horizon, and if so, it may be more costly than the first.

INTRODUCTION

The most difficult task in any relationship is this matter of confrontation. The painful reality of approaching those we love with honesty and openness about damaging personality quirks can be, and often is, excruciating. For most of us, we would rather be the calming voice of compromise than the bold voice of confrontation. Who wants to hurt someone he loves or cares deeply about? Yet what if we could change the life of a family member or a friend for the better, perhaps leading him or her to stronger, more healthy relationships? Why do we allow those we love—and even ourselves—to flounder through life empty, void of any real life change because bringing about that change would require a painful encounter? Why do we steer clear of truth when that truth may heal? Why do we watch those we love systematically ruin any hopes of happiness? Why?

Perhaps it is because we value our position in the relationship more than we value the person. We avoid painful truths that may cost the person in question any real hope of happiness. The bottom line is, we choose to be a hero rather than to be honest. Sad to say, we forget that "trying to help you … helps me" (Blanchard and Miller, 2012, 87). Think about it. Confrontation is, "helping someone see who they really are and the damage they are doing to themselves and others."

Tragically, the one institution that has been placed by God as the divine voice of truth has herself been silenced. The church's confrontational nature has been relegated to a quiet, unobtrusive figure that sits on the periphery of society. Today the body of believers is apologetic and unassuming, her membership grappling with biblical truth and how any Christian can speak those truths into a society that catapults toward depravity. If confrontation is the heartbeat of the church, then we are in cardiac arrest. The loss of this key component will, in the end, kill the church.

CHAPTER 1

Confrontation: What Is It?

S HE WAS SIXTEEN YEARS OLD but smart enough to recognize an inappropriate relationship. She saw her youth pastor and a female volunteer spending time together constantly. In fact, nearly everyone had noticed the innuendos, extended late-night conversations, and constant doting on one another. Added to this was a rumor mill at full throttle. So after much prayer and numerous conversations with her parents, she did what no one else was willing to do: she confronted a man and a woman she loved. The encounter was—you guessed it—less than desirable. Both denied the allegations. Each voiced hurt at such a conclusion and, in time, ostracized and alienated the young woman from her leaders and peers alike. Sad to say, her suspicions turned out to be true, and the end result was two broken marriages, a devastated church, and teenagers who would forever be tainted by the whole ordeal. This sixteen-year-old youth discovered both the high cost of confrontation and the depth of her responsibility in the church.

Warning: So you picked up the book, read the opening paragraph and are now considering a purchase. Let me help, if you want to change your life, your church, and those relationships you hold dear, buy the book. But if you're going to read 2.35 chapters and straighten out everyone, put it down. Killing the Church is dangerous dialogue, conversation which, if mishandled, can result in much heartache.

Though we would admit that confrontation is a part of life, and even more so a component of relationships, it is, in our modern day, a procedure seldom practiced. This ability to share honest dialogue, even in an effort to help another reach his or her potential, is now seen as an invasion of one's privacy.

Mark Twain once described a man who died and met Saint Peter at the pearly gates. Knowing that Saint Peter was very wise, the man asked a question that he had wondered about throughout his life. He said, "Saint Peter, I have been interested in military history for many years. Who was the greatest general of all times?"

Saint Peter quickly responded, "Oh, that's a simple question. It's that man right over there."

"You must be mistaken," responded the man, now very perplexed. "I knew that man on earth, and he was just a common laborer."

"That's right, my friend," assured Saint Peter. "He would have been the greatest general of all time, if he had been a general."

Tom Rath, who shares this story in his book, *Strength 2.0,* goes on to conclude, "This story illustrates a truth that is, unfortunately, all too common. Far too many people spend a lifetime headed in the wrong direction. They go from the cradle to the cubicle and then to the casket, without uncovering their greatest talents and potential" (Rath, 2011, 29–30). Rath is right; too many of us do spend a lifetime headed in the wrong direction. And what's worse, we who love such people never open our mouths. We watch them make their journeys, and we never confront them. What may be more tragic is that the church appears to be doing the same. Think about it: an institution that by her very nature is called to be confrontational is strangely silent. Beyond that, if she does not find her voice, then we all lose.

In fact, let's stop here and make this personal. In what form does confrontation come into your life? To illustrate, let me ask you another question: Do you have any "voices of truth" in your life? Do you have any person or persons to whom you listen for the truth about who you are? For instance, are there certain people to whom you allow the freedom to invade (to confront) your life with observations about how you handle relationships, how you respond to people, your opinions, attitudes, dispositions, and so on? Is there someone—anyone you have given the right to examine your personality—who notes areas that are counterproductive? Keep in mind that these voices are there to keep us accountable and to ensure that we will mature into productive members of both the church and society. But again, do you have anyone who can be brutally honest with you—*about* you? Is anyone honest about personality traits that may be harmful to your ability to build healthy and lasting relationships or even to achieve God's purpose for your life?

For example, most married couples reading at this point would answer, "My spouse is my voice of truth." After thirty-plus years as a marriage counselor, I have discovered that this is often not the case. The vast majority of couples may try in the beginning to be honest and open, but over time they give up. Why? Because early in marriage a pattern develops that frustrates real life change. For instance, the wife may note a personality quirk in her husband that is damaging not only their relationship but also their family life, friendships, work experiences, and so on. Yet every time she attempts to confront the behavior, the husband gets angry, responds by exclaiming, "That's just the way I am!" and then goes off to console his wounded ego. Over time she learns to tolerate the behavior and avoid the confrontation because of the storm that ensues. The same is true of a wife, only her mode of denial may be in another form: tears. The husband seeks to address a certain behavior in his wife that is damaging only to be met by an emotional meltdown.

I heard of two neighbors who were talking over the fence.

"I went to a wedding this weekend," said one, "but I don't think the marriage will last."

"Why not?" asked the other.

"Well, when the groom said 'I do,' the bride said, 'Don't use that tone of voice with me.'"

Regardless of whether one looks at men or women, the result is much the same: there is no real change in either of them. Both learn to live with the behavior and settle down into a level of tolerance that hinders any real hope for intimacy. This is sad, because relationships void of honest dialogue are robbed of the deepest level of companionship. Tragically, most marriages remain stuck at this point, unless an outside entity introduces other "voices of truth" into their life together. But then the question becomes, where will those voices come from?

Some voices of truth come from authority figures that can invade our lives, make observations and recommendations, and then threaten us if we ignore them. For example, an employer can note a damaging personality trait that undermines the purpose of an institution and demand correction or else—where the "or else" is termination of employment. Teachers can also do the same, especially in the elementary grades, but if the parent seeks to defend the child, excusing the behavior, then the child will make little—if any—real change. It is amazing how early in their lives we teach children to see voices of truth as sinister and demeaning, when in reality, the very reason we ought to send them to school is to hear such voices. The purpose of teachers is to assist the parents in developing their children into mature, responsible adults. When, however, a voice of truth or confrontation occurs and hurts our child, we have a tendency to run, coddling and reassuring, to his or her aid. If this is not bad enough, we often side with the child, perhaps enjoying the camaraderie at the expense of real life change.

This can happen as well with employers and other authority figures. A husband comes home and complains about his boss and the dressing-down he got at work. The wife, who may in fact agree with the observation, sides with her husband for the sake of expediency and robs him of any real life change. Tragically, couples live their lives cheated out of any real personality transformation, and they settle down into an existence of mediocrity. Why? Because over time we systematically silence those confrontational figures in our lives.

The same could be said of the church and her authority. People settle into a church home and soon are involved in relationships. At the same time, they begin to hear voices of truth, but instead of accepting the hard, Scriptural truths and adapting their lives accordingly, they instead move their memberships. We tend either to silence voices of truth or to run from them. In fact, this may account for the high number of members who seldom read the Scriptures (the supreme voice of truth) and thereby deny its authority in their lives.

In a book titled *The Success Principles*, Jack Canfield shares an observation critical to our discussion and why we must seek out confrontation rather than avoid it. Canfield states, "To reach your goals more quickly, you need to welcome, receive, and embrace all the feedback that comes your way." Warning! Pastors are not exempt, nor should any authority figure be. Authority figures must not silence those voices of truth in their own lives. Canfield shares a process by which he teaches the principle of goals and feedback in his training seminars. He chooses a volunteer who serves as a representative of a goal in Jack's life. He places the person across the room and then blindfolds himself. The person who represents his goal will either respond with "on course" or "off course" as Jack navigates the room toward his goal.

After the lesson, he asks his audience, "Which did you hear the most?" They respond, "Off course."

He concludes, "The answer is always 'Off course.' And here is the interesting part. I was off course more than I was on course, and I still got there ... just by continually taking action and constantly adjusting to the feedback. The same is true in life. All we have to do is to start to take action and respond to the feedback. If we do that diligently enough and long enough, we will eventually get to our goals and achieve our dreams" (Canfield, 2005, 154).

Canfield is right, and yet I wondered, what if there are no voices saying *off course*? What if we silence or demand that those voices be quiet? How many people are wandering through life and shutting out the voices that may be shouting *off course*? What happens if we never allow confrontational voices to be heard and we cheat ourselves of the opportunity to reach our goals? Worse, what if we choose to be silent when those we love are tragically off course and failing in their goals? Canfield continues, "So, as you can see, when someone gives you feedback, there are three possible reactions that don't work: (1) crying, falling apart, caving in, and giving up; (2) getting angry at the source of the feedback; and (3) not listening to or ignoring the feedback" (Canfield, 2005, 154).

Let me add a fourth possibility: *never allowing the feedback to begin with.* In other words, if I am off course, then I don't want to know it. Just keep your mouth shut and let me find my own way across the room. The only problem is that for many of us, we never find our way across the room. Going back to Canfield's illustration, we never reach our goals, and thereby we die in the room, wandering.

Why is this important to preachers? Because we have been ordained by God to be those voices that cry out, "Off course." Moreover, we are to teach the body of believers how to *give* feedback as well as receive it. For instance, Canfield concludes, "Most people will not voluntarily give you feedback. They are as uncomfortable with possible confrontation as you are. They don't want to hurt your feelings. They are afraid of your reaction … so to get honest and open feedback, you are going to need to ask for it … and make it safe for the person to give it to you … Don't shoot the messenger" (Canfield, 2005, 154). When I read that, I thought, *How sad that the church and her leadership are becoming increasingly uncomfortable with this task of confrontation.* Confrontation is the voice that says to us all, "Off course."

If there is any responsibility of the church, it is to confront people. Confrontation is an intricate part of life and a valuable tool in keeping us on course in relationships and with goals. But there's more. Not only are we reluctant to receive confrontational voices, but we are also uncomfortable about being one. Why? Many of us we think, *Who am I to confront anyone about his or her life when I can barely manage my own life?"* This reminds me of the little boy who tearfully asked his mother after a rather vigorous spanking, "Mom, how do you make yourself do what you ought to do?"

Is that not the real issue of our lives: how we manage ourselves? And even deeper than that: who out there will help us? Who will confront us, help us, and manage us? And will I let them? Harold Walker states, "There is more than a hint of our human predicament in the cartoon strip *Dennis the Menace.* Hank Ketchum came home from work one evening and found his wife suffering from exasperation only a mother can know. "Hank," she said to her husband, "our son Dennis is a menace."

Harold Walker, who wrote the book *How to Manage Yourself*, went on to say, "Sometimes we wonder if Dennis will ever grow from menace to manhood, from immaturity to maturity" (Walker, 1955, 5).

Don't we sometimes wonder if *we* will ever grow from menace to manhood? In fact, who confronts anyone anymore about anything? What confrontational voices are there in the church or in our lives that guide us on this pilgrimage of spiritual maturity, which should be our goal as believers in Christ? Who will love us enough to confront us? Who will help us manage our lives and reach our goals of being Christlike? Will we even let them?

And how about the confronter? For example, the youth mentioned earlier faced the difficult task of confrontation. Is her courage to confront the tool for helping all of us manage our lives? Is there a responsibility we share to help others do the same? Could confrontation be a discipline of the faith that has been discarded, or is it an attribute no longer relevant to our day?

In fact, our courageous youth in the introduction reminded me of a conversation I had with a pastor who met with his leadership one evening in a let's-be-honest meeting. His concern was over a membership that was, in his opinion, apathetic and indifferent; the church was barely surviving. He said, "We discussed, argued, and hashed over the low numbers, the lack of commitment, and worst of all, the ungodly lifestyles of our members. After we spent most of the night in deliberation, our assessment was simple: we were dying, and the cost to confront our members and fix the problem was too great."

Wow! He admitted what many pastors and leaders are coming to realize—that to confront people about their lifestyles or any component of their lives, especially in relation to the disciplines of our faith, can be excruciating. Yet, as in the case of Dennis the Menace, if he and his leaders are not willing, then who will be? Who will move this church—or for that matter, anyone—from menace to manhood, from immaturity to maturity? In essence, who will confront the membership with the truth, and risk the repercussions?

When I pressed the pastor, he admitted to being afraid. He said, "I feel like a parent who has been negligent in child rearing and wakes to find that his sweet little toddler has evolved into a rebellious teenager." We are in a crisis. We are desperately trying to incorporate a form of correction when we may already have waited too late. In fact, after raising four children of my own, I understood exactly what he was saying. When a parent chooses to exercise little guidance and discipline in the early years of their child's development and then later seeks to do so, they are in for a rough ride.

His crisis is our crisis. Church authorities are finally waking up to find rebellious members occupying the house. Some might ask: But why the fear? Because parents and pastors both understand that to attempt any form of correction after years of neglect can and will be a gut-wrenching experience. In the case of church, family, or business—or for that matter, any relationship—correction that comes late will usually take a much heavier toll on all those involved. In other words, anytime you allow someone in a relationship to live with little guidance as to his or her responsibilities within that relationship and then later try to incorporate discipline, your task will be tough.

What does this mean to the church? The cost of confrontation and correction may threaten the survival of some churches, and yet failure to do so may undermine the very reason for which they exist: the Great Commission. Some leaders are already recognizing that confrontation may be the hardest battle waged in Christendom since the reformation. Churches and perhaps even denominations may cease to exist. Why? Because many individuals will not respond in a positive way to confrontation, let alone correction. But it is here that we must ask ourselves the question: "Can we refuse to confront because people don't want it?"

How did we get to this point? How do relationships—and for that matter, churches—end up with growing numbers of participants who are undisciplined and out-of-control? Church members look more like Dennis the Menace than appendages of the body of Christ. What has brought about this evolution of the church that has resulted in a constituency that votes based on economics rather than ethics—parishioners who can sing "Amazing Grace" on Sunday and trample the blood of Christ in an election booth on Tuesday? Where are the strong voices that are not afraid to confront and say to their congregations, "Off course"?

Killing the church is not to be seen as an attack against the church any more than discipline is an attack against a child. The reality is that without correction little can be done to keep child or church on course. And for correction to be effective, it first requires confrontation.

Confrontation is never easy and at times can be very laborious. Ask any parent of a defiant teenager who has sat up till the early morning hours, stood in the driveway, and then mustered up all the courage they had to confront the rebellion. Ask any parent who is forced to say after years of negligence, "You will have to live within the rules and guidelines of this home." Let's admit it; by the time parents reach this point, they are crippled by fear and intimidated into silence—crippled because they are consumed by how their child will respond. Will he blow up and rebel further by jumping into the car, racing away into even greater acts of defiance? Will she become so irate as to explode into a verbal or, worse, physical barrage? Or will this young person quietly go to his room where, moments later, the parent will hear a gunshot or find him in a comatose state with a pill bottle by his side?

Every parent understands the dilemma of anyone in authority when it comes to confronting. In fact, let's be honest; fear can cause any authority figure to back off and be intimidated into saying or doing nothing. So the result is that many churches are failing in this parental role, suckered by rebellious, immature members who challenge the leadership with blatant misbehavior. Church leaders are not, like some parents, out in the driveway. Instead they are locked away in the back bedroom where out-of-sight is out-of-mind and what they don't know won't hurt them. The outcome is this: we have created a kinder, gentler church that compromises her mission, a church where ministers, like many parents, have given up their God-given responsibility in an attempt to be a buddy rather than a parent, letting their charges live as they choose.

This book is a pilgrimage, a journey through the controversial and unpleasant subject of confrontation. May you and I be moved through these pages to genuine repentance. Remember the words of Peter: "For it is time for judgment to begin with the family of God" (1 Peter 4:17 NIV). May we understand that what is killing the church may also be threatening our nation. In other words, we could be yielding territory to the enemy, loading the weapons of our critics with the bullets we have provided, and parading an adulterated bride who undermines both the Great Commission and the purpose of the church and desperately needs to be confronted. The truth is, those of other beliefs need not look far to find slander and accusations to throw at her. For we, the church, have provided all they need. While strict guidelines and a deep level of commitment govern many of the world's religions, we have forgotten the disciplines of our own faith. The church has rewritten the mandates, polished the demands into suggestions, and there is little concern for righteous living. Consequently, we may threaten to destroy our own land far more effectively than the cowardly terrorists who fly planes into buildings. We have forgotten that historically our righteous living has always been a stranglehold on our critic; our changed lives silence those who would otherwise lash out at our faith.

So what are we to do? Perhaps like a ball team in the locker room we must return to the field with a new level of abandonment. May we be the player who rallies the team, not afraid to get in the face of our fellow members, spurring them on to excellence, never allowing the game to be threatened by a shoddy, halfhearted effort. May we be willing to confront.

Recently I took my kayak and camping gear and spent a couple of days clearing my head. While picking up supplies at the local Walmart, I came across a small book entitled *The Difference Maker* by John Maxwell. In a section dealing with problems, he states, "One of the reasons that problem solving is so difficult is that we are often too close to the problems to truly understand them" (Maxwell, 2006, 102). Perhaps this is true of the church too; maybe we are too close to the problem to truly understand it.

Further, maybe pastors and church leaders have stood closer to the congregation than we have to Christ. If anything is to change, then leadership and laity must step back from the church and be guided by the Holy Sprit to see the problem. To see the crisis from the eyes of anyone other than Christ is to magnify it rather than to solve it. However, to get the perspective of Christ, we must see the prayer closet as the critical ingredient to effective confrontation. Again, if we do otherwise, we will endanger the Great Commission. Maxwell went on to share cartoonist Ashleigh Brilliant's remark: "I don't have any solutions, but I certainly admire the problem" (Maxwell, 2006, 102). For many in positions of leadership there is a type of admiration by which the church can talk about her problems without ever solving them. Even preaching about a problem without any attempt to solve it is merely "admiring it."

Helping the Laity

For the laity there will be an added section at the end of each chapter entitled, "Helping the Laity." This portion will ensure that the work is not merely the tool of church leaders but of the laity as well. The purpose will be to assist the membership in learning how to apply the principles to their own lives and their attempts to confront within their relationships outside the church. Keep in mind that there is the danger of people seeing this as a reason to assault others. In fact, it is critical to any form of confrontation that those to whom the task may fall will not do so with brutality but rather with grace and wisdom. To do otherwise is to undermine the church through cruelty, which in the final outcome could destroy her witness as effectively as the very lifestyles she wishes to confront. In fact, I have been so fearful of such a reaction that there were times I debated on writing this book at all. The church cannot survive the misguided attempts of unspiritual people who grab their Bibles and barge into the lives of others with no Scriptural framework from which to work. My apprehension is that members of the body of Christ will read a couple of chapters and then feel equipped to go out and invade the lives of others, attempting to do what must be bathed in prayer and guided by the Holy Spirit.

CHAPTER 2

Church: A Place of Confrontation

Robert F. Johnson, age fifty-five, was found dead in the lobby of Southwest General Health Center, a hospital in Middleburg Heights, Ohio. Imagine that. He was not in the ER or on the operating table but in the lobby. Surrounded by the latest technological advances, in the company of trained personnel, he died in the lounge area. All the expertise to address his condition was available, yet his life ended within the very institution established to help. This man did not come in and ask for assistance or fill out a list of forms; he simply came in and sat down and died. Did he have any idea how sick he was? Did anyone stop to note his condition, or did he just blend in, camouflaged into the decor of the waiting room? Did Mr. Johnson know how close he was to the end? Why was he not in a coffee shop or a bookstore? Why a hospital? Why did he die? He died because no one bothered to stop and ask him, "Are you sick?" People filed past, not wanting to disturb him. They kept quiet because they thought he was asleep. No, he wasn't asleep. He was dead. No one took time to stop and confront his condition.

Though we may never know why Mr. Johnson chose to die in a hospital lobby, perhaps he represents multitudes in the church who wander into the membership unchanged, content to sit in the foyer of commitment, like parishioners who take up space in the auditorium but are, at best, spiritually sick, or at worst, dead. These are men and women who meander in and out of local congregations, desperately in need of confrontation. Congregants have discovered that the best place to hide their spiritual condition is in the church. Leaders wake up to find members who, like Mr. Johnson, are in the vestibules of their churches, their conditions serious, and few—if any—are willing to stop and conduct an examination.

Why? Because they fear confrontation, a condition that today plagues both the leadership and the laity. This apprehension has created leadership who tiptoe through the sanctuary, forgetting that a corpse in the church is as negative as a cadaver in the lobby of a hospital. Think about it: a church is by her nature confrontational, and so too are those who lead her. Yet today we have a growing reluctance to confront anyone about anything.

Imagine a medical community where doctors never want to confront a patient with a dangerous, life threatening lifestyle, where men and women are too afraid to address an illness and provide personal counsel. In fact, how many times has a doctor hurt your feelings by telling you the truth, not in a generic way by announcing it to the waiting room but to you, personally. For example, a doctor looks at you and says, "You are too heavy, and you need to quit eating sweets." His confrontational manner results in you making real lifestyle changes. I remember, after my return to the States, a doctor who was so bold as to say to me, "If you are not going to listen to my counsel, then don't waste my time." Wow, talk about confrontational.

We go to a doctor or enter a hospital with the understanding that we will be confronted with truth about our physical bodies, regardless of how painful the information might be. Yet today's church, a place we go for our spiritual bodies—as some would say, "a hospital for sinners"—is losing her confrontational edge. She is surrounded by death, frightened into silence, and is in danger of crashing. Why? Her cargo threatens her very purpose. In fact, I read a humorous story of a couple of hunters who illustrate the problem.

> Two hunters got a pilot to fly them into the far north for
> elk hunting. They were quite successful in their venture and

bagged four big bucks. The pilot came back, as arranged, to pick them up. They started loading their gear into the plane, including the four elk. But the pilot objected and said, "The plane can only take two of your elk; you will have to leave two behind." They argued with him, since the year before they had shot four and the pilot had allowed them to put all aboard. The plane was the same model and capacity.

Reluctantly, the pilot finally permitted them to bring all four aboard. But when they attempted to take off and leave the valley, the little plane couldn't make it, and they crashed into the wilderness.

Climbing out of the wreckage, one hunter said to the other, "Do you know where we are?"

"I think so," the other hunter replied. "I think this is about the same place we crashed last year."

How did the church evolve from hospital to museum? Why are so many local churches descending, losing altitude, plummeting toward their ruin? After nearly thirty-five years in ministry and much research, I believe it all starts with how the average man or woman not only views the local church but, more so, how they join it. For example, our hunters' problem started the moment they boarded. Today, most people unite with a church as if they were climbing on board a cruise ship. They walk the aisle, which usually means moving their membership, stow their gear, grab a deck chair, and wait to be served. They forget that the very purpose of the church is for their spiritual health.

What's worse is that they can begin to look like some of the crowds Jesus had around him. John 6:66 says, "From this time many of his disciples turned back and no longer followed him." Why? These were men and women who had followed Jesus for a happy meal and would have continued to do so had it not been for the confrontational "hard sayings" of Christ. The crowds of the New Testament were like many church members today, content to meander along with Jesus, standing on the periphery, unchanged and unconcerned, along for the ride.

Killing the Church

Max Lucado states, "God has enlisted us in his navy and placed us on his ship. The boat has one purpose—to carry us to the other shore. This is no cruise ship; it's a battleship. We aren't called to a life of leisure; we are called to a life of service" (Lucado, 1996, 160). In other words, if people come to church as if they were climbing on board a cruise ship, then it is logical that they don't expect or appreciate confrontation. Instead, they expect to relax, unwind, and be served. If the captain or staff of the ship were to come up and begin to examine or, worse, address their lifestyle or the choices they made at the buffet, then they would become irate and most likely determine to use another cruise line in the future. Huh. This sounds like church members today.

What's wrong here? The church either failed to educate her constituents when they first boarded or else she compromised her mission in order to get them to board at all. You may want to read that sentence and chew on it awhile. Again, what went wrong? The church forgot to tell people, "This is a place of confrontation." In other words, they are in the business of examination and invading the personal lives of those who choose to join them. Yet today, the masses unite without being told what the church is about and, moreover, what she expects out of them.

In a critical way, what's happening to the body of believers is the equivalent of someone mistakenly walking into a hospital or a doctor's office and thinking they are on a cruise ship. Imagine coming into a hospital lobby, putting on some suntan lotion, slipping on your shades, sipping on a drink, and asking a nurse when the dance starts? Multitudes are joining the church in much the same manner. In other words, the church is called to examine its members' spiritual conditions just like a hospital deals with people's physical conditions.

Jesus not only understood this propensity of people for leisure rather than service; he was a master at confronting it. He recognized that many in the crowd were caught up in the emotion of the moment and would scatter when there was a cost to following him. So he refused to allow people to join up without confronting them about that cost. In fact, this is what the Lord referred to when he spoke of a type of soil that receives the Word with joy but never allows it to take root. He warned his followers of these tagalongs for whom the world has a low tolerance. Jesus knew the danger of "unsalty saints," extremities in the body who lacked any resemblance to the head and were, in fact, not part of the body at all. These are church members who live in habitual disobedience with little regard, if any, to the teachings of Scripture—spiritual zombies who become angry when you do address them. This is a segment of the church that is not only growing stronger but also louder. They live defiantly with no accountability and no one bold enough to confront them. Jesus warned us that an institution infected in this way, if left to itself, would be "trampled underfoot." Confrontation is a responsibility of the church that should begin the moment a person enters the building. If a church fails to grasp this, then the result will be a crowd rather than a congregation. Remember: once churches gravitate away from spiritual hospitals to cruise ships, they begin to see people as consumers rather than congregants. What's worse, they develop a competitive spirit toward other churches/cruise ships.

Jesus warned his followers of the damage of "unsalty saints," those men and women who have joined up for the amenities, perks, and privileges. In fact, we may be witnessing the fulfillment of his warning in our nation and perhaps even in other parts of the world—a contempt for the church. Why? Like egg white that is tasteless or a piece of meat that is spoiling for lack of salt, America plummets to depravity while she tramples an anemic church under her well-worn path. The church is strong numerically but floundering spiritually. It has grown in membership yet fails to confront disobedience. The church is no longer a place of confrontation.

The outcome is an ecclesiastical structure that is being tossed out of our society, from the classroom to the courtroom. Why? The bride of Christ is demanding that the Ten Commandments remain at the courthouse, while the world has been watching her disregard that same law in the church house. She has failed to teach, to confront, to hold accountable her membership to the very disciplines she espouses. People join with little, if any, accountability. *Christianity Today*, in an article entitled "Fixing Church Discipline," reminds us that "the protestant reformers named three marks by which the true church is known: the preaching of the pure doctrine of the gospel, the pure administration of the sacraments, and the exercise of church discipline to correct faults" (Jeschke, 2005, 31). Let me add that this is not a book about discipline—though it is sure to come up—but rather, confrontation. Is there a difference? Yes, because without confrontation, there is no discipline. If the church is to regain her mooring, she must know the necessity of the first over the second. We may falter over methodology and approach in discipline, but confrontation is another matter.

Tragically, if the church neglects confrontation, the front line of accountability, she begins to look more like a "kept woman" than a victorious bride. Her leadership avoids confrontation and instead becomes consumed with buildings and budgets rather than changed lives. Clergy forget purity and instead are enamored with ecclesiastical laurels. They toy with the inclination of the masses to identify with Christ without a true conversion experience. There is a propensity that corrupts the church's effectiveness and, given time, compromises her integrity, thereby diluting her preservative quality. Ultimately, her mission is squandered and her only cure is leaders who are reluctant to confront. The outcome is that the lobby continues to fill up. As John MacArthur put it, "A church that does not mourn over sin, especially sin within its fellowship, is on the edge of spiritual disaster" (MacArthur, 1984, 122–23, 275). I believe that disaster has already arrived. Perhaps a true story told to me may illustrate better this reality. I have made some changes to protect the parties involved.

> A teenager, unable to sleep, gets up and walks into the living room, only to discover his dad glued to a porn photo on the computer screen. Unbeknownst to the father, his son in a single moment not only leaves the room feeling betrayed but, worse, abandons Christianity for the next twenty years. Tragically, this dad never knew about his son's discovery. A father and son's relationship was severed

by actions about which the parent had no idea. For all this dad knew, his private sin was undiscovered. The disaster continued until a holiday gathering, when a brave daughter-in-law confronted her self-righteous father-in-law with his double life and the effect that it had on her husband and his own son. Her willingness to expose the dark secret was her attempt to reconcile the two.

As I listened to the story, I thought that the real tragedy was that the dad had lived for years wondering why his son cared so little for his faith. But maybe this story illustrates the growing disdain of the nation and the world toward the church? Is it possible that nonbelievers have been gazing over the shoulder of the average membership, growing nauseated by what they see? Members have forgotten that their lifestyle may be the greatest hindrance to accomplishing the Great Commission, and the church is too afraid to confront. Christ warned in Matthew 5:13, "You are the salt of the earth. But if the salt loses its saltiness, how can it be made salty again? It is no longer good for anything, except to be thrown out and trampled by men under foot." When the church is robbed of confrontation, when her authority figures choose to remain silent in the presence of gross disobedience, then respect is lost.

William Whiston was a theological figure during the days of King George II and was also a favorite to Queen Caroline. On one occasion, the queen questioned Whiston as to some area of her life that she might seek to correct and make more conducive to the teachings of Christ. He responded, "Madam, since you ask me this question, I will tell you. When you come into the chapel, I notice that you do not pay proper reverence but instead whisper and make signs to those women around you. This sets a bad example for the rest of the congregation." The queen accepted his counsel about her lack of reverence (Hastings, 1978, 228).

Wow! Here the queen of England was admonished by a lowly religious figure. Not only did she receive his rebuke, but she asked him for it. Voices of truth are critical to our lives if there are to be any real and lasting changes. The church is a place of relationships and truth and is a place to encounter that truth.

Helping the Laity: Relationships as a Place of Confrontation

Any relationship can and should be a place of confrontation. In other words, no relationship can be healthy and fulfilling if there is not honesty and truth. For example, if you are in a friendship that does not allow for candid dialogue, then you will be a frustrated friend. Sad to say, there are multitudes of men and women who are wandering in and out of friendships, marriages, and relationships with little, if any, depth or understanding as to how they work. Like Mr. Johnson, they resemble a corpse more than an intricate part of a life-changing companionship. Many are aware that something is wrong, but they don't know how to fix it. They confess an inability to maintain a real connection with anyone. Their marriages, like their friendships, are marked with stress and frustration. Why? Because there is no honest dialogue in the form of confrontation. And because of this, they never recognize or come to terms with their own weaknesses. Therefore, they bail out of one relationship and migrate to another. Pastors can do this by continually moving from one church to the next. Members do the same when they meet with confrontation.

Tragically, people go through life, laboring to develop an affinity with anyone. They admit there is a crisis, but they lack the wisdom to know how to address it. They wander into the foyer of commitment but go no further, because they know already what is waiting in the other rooms. I am convinced, after thirty years of counseling, that many neither grasp nor understand how intimacy is developed. And intimacy can never happen without confrontation. Honesty and openness are stumped by abrasive personality traits that desperately need to be confronted but are never addressed. Confrontation is a frightening undertaking. Even as I sat working on this manuscript, a man entered a coffee shop with a T-shirt that read, "It's better to have loved and lost than to live with a psycho the rest of your life." No doubt he had experienced some heartache along the way. Sad to say, he may have ended a marriage because neither he nor his wife could be honest and address (confront) the real issues.

You may be asking yourself, "How can a book that tackles the dynamics of relationships within the church help in all other relationships?" Think about it. Who better to study than the Creator as he maintains an intimate association with his creation through His church? If the body of believers can solve her problems, it will no doubt trickle down to every relationship. However, to do so requires that we understand and develop the skills of confrontation. Again, keep in mind that if one is struggling in relationships and yet refuses any form of confrontation, they are destined to fail. In other words, if we are stubborn and unyielding, angrily retaliating at anyone who gets in our face with the truth, then we must not be surprised by failure. Voices of truth are critical to relationships, and to stifle honesty is to damage any hope of the deepest level of camaraderie.

My daughter texted her husband during a service and said, "I am under conviction, and it feels so good."

A pastor who was somewhat of a role model in my early years of ministry used to say, "When people leave a service, they should be mad, sad, or glad." He went on to explain that the real tragedy comes when men and women can leave a church and feel none of the above. The church, like any relationship, should be a place of confrontation.

CHAPTER 3

Pastor: A Person of Confrontation

"**P**ASTOR, HELP ME FIX MY marriage."

Twenty minutes into the session it was evident that what she was asking would require a level of honesty on my part that I wasn't sure she could handle. I tried to counsel, delving into critical issues, but her hidden, destructive personality was coming to the surface like a submarine for battle. She was getting on my nerves in the first ten minutes of the session. I thought, *Poor husband. Poor family. Poor me."* Confrontation in this case would be ugly and horribly painful. (The conclusion of the story is at the end of this chapter.)

This woman reminded me of a story I read about a couple who had to interrupt their vacation to go to the dentist. "I want a tooth pulled, and I don't want any pain shots or novocaine because I'm in a big hurry," the woman said. "Just yank out the tooth as quickly as possible, and we'll be on our way." The dentist was quite impressed. "You're certainly a courageous woman," he said. "Which tooth is it?" The woman turned to her husband and said, "Show him your tooth, dear" (Krauss, 2012, 2).

If the assumption in the previous chapter is correct and the church is a place of confrontation, then so too are the relationships of the ones who lead her. If this is true, why is there so little confrontation in the church? Are today's church leaders so seduced by the benefits and power that come to their position that they have given up their God-given responsibility to be honest? In other words, though they are called by God to be voices of truth, they instead get caught up in recognition, doting over denominational notice. They are clergy who admit that some of their church growth is questionably induced, but they give in to the lure of an ever-increasing membership. One pastor said as much when he admitted, "It looks good on the records."

Wow! Think about that. It would be like a cancer patient bragging that their tumor has gotten larger! Tragically, Satan coaxes the leaders of these congregational cruise ships into undermining purity with popularity. Like the disciples arguing over who was the greatest, these guides gather to gloat over recognition based on results rather than repentance. They corral weekly an overweight, spiritually lazy congregation, who are content to recline on the sofa of satisfaction, sipping the tea of tolerance, and all of it occurs—you guessed it—in the waiting room of the church. They may have increasing numbers but little, if any, confrontation and accountability. These are members who resemble a crowd rather than a congregation. They are congregants who come for relationships without responsibility, patrons who enter churches the way they enter malls—as *consumers*. They show up every week to take rather than to give.

Imagine a department store where people come in, choose what items they like, and carry them out the door without paying—and to make matters worse, the management is too frightened to confront them. You might argue, "But that's different; grace is free." You're right. Grace has no price tag, but the cost of identifying with its founder does, and multitudes are joining, oblivious to that cost. The church is crippled by the caliber of leaders who may be unwilling to confront, fearing the loss of members and revenue. For example, I feared the woman at the beginning of this chapter. Why? She and her husband were key leaders and systematic givers, and they held numerous positions. My honesty with her could jeopardize their continued status within the fellowship. Yet failure to confront her could possibly destroy her marriage, family, and the church. What did I love more: her or her contributions?

To many, a confrontational leader—especially a pastor—sounds harsh. It shouldn't. Charles Swindoll said of leaders, "Leadership is necessary. Leaders are the ones who dream the dreams. Leaders are the ones who are the visionaries. They are the ones that have to answer the hardest questions within the outfit. They deal with the most complicated of issues. There is both risk and exhilaration in the full view that they have in mind, for they are the ones that are out front and continually address the perspective, where we are going" (Swindoll, 1998, 333).

Jesus lived this out, constantly demonstrating the strongest call to integrity by confronting those who wished to join up without weighing the cost. In fact, He continually challenged the shallow sojourners who sought to slip in without identifying with the cause. At the beginning of Jesus' ministry, he had crowds—multitudes who were enamored by his teaching, clamoring along like starry-eyed eighteen-year-olds gazing at a recruiting poster. The problem was that they were oblivious to the spiritual war in progress. They were would-be soldiers, followers who desired dynasties without discipline, relationships without rules.

Think about it. Imagine if today's military were run like the average church—soldiers enlisting with no accountability, attending drills if and when they chose, drifting from one unit to the next. There would be no drill instructors, no exercise, and no mandatory attendance, just an army where the soldier could do as he pleased. To the leaders of such forces, that scenario would be a nightmare. Leaders must be confrontational if they are to be effective, pastors included.

Jesus taught his disciples by example that nothing involving people—not even the church—could be effective if there was no accountability, discipline, and confrontation. He was a master at confronting and would not allow disobedience or shallowness to go unnoticed. Yet today's leaders and pastors often flounder with this quality and are afraid to exercise this discipline of the church. Some pastors are convinced that it is impossible to hold up the standard of the institution and do so with grace, while others wrestle with the belief that it is not a part of their role as a pastor. There are a number of clergy who seem to think that members should be allowed to find their own way. They argue, "This is the role and responsibility of the Holy Spirit, not the pastor." In an attempt to understand that logic, let me pull a page from my journal during my missionary days in Zimbabwe, Africa.

In 1991 we were a family of six, fresh on the mission field and horribly lonely. Christmas came only weeks after we had arrived and, to be honest, the prospects of surviving our first holidays overseas seemed dim. So, in an effort to divert our homesickness, we did what most missionaries do: we played tourist. Teaming up with dear friends, we traveled to one of the wonders of the natural world, Victoria Falls. It is a place between Zimbabwe and Zambia where the Zambezi River falls with such force that it catapults a liquid avalanche of mist toward the heavens and finally onto the heads of all who travel her rim.

On this first visit, our four children—ages five to twelve—were strong-willed. Each pulled in the direction of the crevice, jockeying for position, begging me to let them get closer. Even as I write this, my skin crawls. Why? While they were pulling away, I was squeezing their hands with all my might. The closer we came to the edge, the harder I squeezed. Why react in this manner? Why not just let them find their own way, live the adventure, make their own pilgrimage? First, I recognized the danger. Second, I recognized the immaturity of my children. Third, I understood my guardianship and responsibility to their well-being. Imagine if I had simply called out behind them, "Be careful," or worse yet, "You're on your own." You would recommend a more responsible guardian. Yet how many church members dance on the edge of a much deeper spiritual chasm with little if any concern or confrontation by the very authority figures in charge.

Let me illustrate. Take a moment and draw a stick man with a big smile on his face inside of a box. After you finish, write, "the counsel of Scripture" along the outer perimeter of the box. Now, once you have completed the first box, draw a second box just like the first. Again, write "the counsel of Scripture" around each of the four sides, but this time put the stick man outside the box with a sad face. Now take some time to study the illustration and write down your initial thoughts. What conclusions did you come to? Why does the man inside the box have a happy face, while the man outside the box has a sad one?

Here we have a picture of a single life anchored in God's word, focused on God's will, obedient to God's commands, and enjoying the blessings and protection of God. In other words, our joyful little sojourner has boundaries established by God, and because he lives within those boundaries, he is content. The second picture reflects our same little pilgrim, only this time he has moved outside the box and will most likely feel the disciplinary hand of God. This is the reason for the frown. However, the question then becomes: in what form does God's correction come? How does God confront our little stick man? What is the pastor's role in the case of the one who lives outside of the box? Further, what hope does anyone have if the leadership chooses to remain neutral?

Some pastors seem to be convinced that their parishioners will eventually come to their senses and find their own way back inside the box. Perhaps this is where the contemporary church has been duped by the enemy into thinking that the leadership should just maintain a low profile and wait for immature members to come to their senses. Do you realize how much damage our little man can do to himself and others if allowed to wander in disobedience? Instead of confronting apostates who are living outside the tenets of our faith, leaders today are excusing the behavior and watching "comrade sheep" dance on the brink of spiritual disaster. What is the church to do with those who live outside the precepts of God's law?

First, if you're a pastor, let's begin by settling two issues. If God were to bless your little out-of-the-box member, he would, over time, be affirming areas of disobedience rather than reproving them. Os Guinness in his book *Dining with the Devil* states, "If Jesus Christ is the head of the church and hence the source and goal of its entire life, true growth is only possible in obedience to him" (Guinness, 1993, 43). Yet for many leaders in today's church, obedience is seen as a kind of optional lifestyle, an alternative for the more fanatical. In other words, it really doesn't matter if our little man is in or out of the box, as long as he's happy. That's another chapter. The bottom line is, it does matter. The church—and more particularly the leadership—must understand that failing to confront and showering the usual fellowship and privileges on members living in clear violation to the Scripture is reinforcing disobedience.

Think about it this way. When parents, the authority figures, are raising a child and seeks to alter a pattern of undesirable behavior, they will do so by removing privileges and even isolating the child from the rest of the family—in other words, by sending him to his room. Why? They are trying to bring him into line or, in the case of our illustration, get him back into the box.

A mother might say to her child, "If you clean your room this morning, I will take you for ice cream after lunch." If the child is compliant, he is rewarded as promised. Mom understands that this practice, done over time, will lead to the pattern of behavior desired. If, however, the child refuses to obey, then Mom would hold back the privilege and perhaps even reinforce her correction with some form of punishment. The point is that she uses the reward as a bargaining tool in negotiating proper conduct. It would appear from Scripture that God uses much the same pattern when exercising his dominion over his children, and he often incorporates pastoral leadership in the process, as we will see later. But for now, suffice it to say that there is a parental role, be it pastor or parent. There's only one problem. Today's church, and its leaders more so, appear to be taking the noncompliant child or member for ice cream, thereby making God's job more difficult. Because of poor leadership, our little man is having a marvelous time outside the box. He has no desire to move his life back into the realm of obedience. And maybe there is a tendency among leaders to fear those they lead. You might want to read that last sentence again.

John Maxwell tells the story of a census worker in a rural area.

> Driving down the country roads, he saw many houses with "Beware of Dog" signs. At the gate of the last address on his list, he saw another "Beware of Dog" sign as he entered

a farmyard near a barn. Afraid to get out of the car, he honked his horn, and soon a man came out of the barn with a small Chihuahua at his heels. When the census taker was done asking his questions and filling out his paperwork, he mentioned how many beware-of-dog signs he had seen and asked, "Is this the dog all the signs are about?'

"Yup, sure is," the farmer replied, picking up the friendly dog.

"But that dog couldn't keep anyone away."

"I know," said the farmer, "but the signs sure do."

The lesson is that fear is like a warning sign that makes us afraid of a dog that cannot hurt us!" (Maxwell, 2006, 127)

I believe that many clergy are much like that census worker—too afraid to get out of the car and commit to the difficult task of a spiritual census of their own members. Maxwell goes on to say, "Fear makes us afraid of doing something that might be beneficial for us. Taking action will require us to move into the unknown. That can be scary. But if we give in to our fear, we don't move forward" (Maxwell, 2006, 128).

Maxwell's words are even truer when it comes to a pastor and his congregation. If he is reluctant to address disobedience in the life of the membership, he is not the only one who is not moving forward; an entire church may not be moving, either. Many pastors are silenced by Chihuahua members who are not the threat they are perceived to be.

Tom Rieger, who wrote a fascinating book, *Breaking the Fear Barrier*, states, "There are no fearless leaders, but there are courageous ones. Everyone has fears they need to face. The key is to learn to overcome those fears … leaders must master fear—their own and others'. They have to have the courage to fix what's wrong." He goes on to say what I believe may hold many pastors prisoner in the area of confrontation: "The first fear leaders have to face is their own fear of loss" (Rieger, 2011, 121).

The Cost of Confrontation

Churches and leadership must recognize that the cost of turning the church may be great. How great? Congregations who begin to confront and exercise discipline may be unable to continue due to the loss in revenue and personnel. The immediate response to a statement like this is: "Even a corrupt church is better than no church at all." But is that true? Do we honestly believe that a community is better off with a church, regardless of its condition?

Suppose you move your family to a new neighborhood, and your child comes in complaining that they are bored because they have no friends. Over the next couple of weeks, you find them seldom at home and soon discover that they have taken up with an older kid down the street. However, upon investigation you discover that the new friend is involved in drugs, alcohol, and promiscuity. Would your response to your spouse be, "Well, even a corrupt friend is better then no friend at all"? No. In fact, you would seek to distance your child from the culprit.

A church in a depraved condition is damaging to the cause of Christ, and to maintain its survival could do much in the way of harm. So the question becomes: is it beneficial to the cause of Christ for some churches to die? Should we let a church die? The problem with this train of thought is that few believers can accept it. They see the death of a church as contrary to scriptural teaching and a clear desire of the enemy. Is it possible that our enemy would actually enjoy the continued survival of a church? Could God seek the death of a local church for a greater good?

In the case of the church at Laodicea, we find both a strong numerical and financial base. Yet God threatens the church with their continued existence. "I know all the things you do, that you are neither hot nor cold. I wish you were one or the other! But since you are like lukewarm water, I will spit you out of my mouth! You say, 'I am rich. I have everything I want. I don't need a thing!' And you don't realize that you are wretched and miserable and poor and blind and naked" (Revelation 3:15–17 NLT).

Laodicea's testimony was one of great wealth and riches, but her purity had been compromised. In fact, the word *Laodicea* means "the people ruled," and though this congregation took great delight in their achievements, Christ saw their condition as anemic. A people lingering in the fringes of disobedience, He counsels the church with a strong warning, "I will spit you out" (Revelation 3:16 NLT). Why? Christ reminds this congregation that the testimony of the kingdom and the Great Commission would be better served if they did not exist at all. Again, this was a church that had, for all practical purposes, evolved into an offense to the cause of Christ by her blemished condition. Too many today have the opinion that a church's mere presence is a good thing, yet when that existence becomes a barrier, blocking would-be converts, then the world might be better off without it. The bottom line is this: a membership that refuses biblical confrontation and discipline compromises the Great Commission and places the task solely on the pastor's shoulders. When this happens, there is usually a premature end to an otherwise competent ministry.

The Cost of Confrontation in the Life of a Pastor

Pastor Larry was young in age and experience, three years out of seminary, and now in a precarious situation. The chairman of deacons had been seen in a topless bar in the capital city with a group of businessmen. Troubled by his youth joking over the matter had only made the situation worse. He and his wife knew that to address the issue would result in tough times, yet not to do so went against all they stood for. So, one Sunday afternoon he went to the deacon's home, confronting him with the facts and asking for his resignation. If you're a pastor reading this, do you want to guess what happened? Within two weeks, the chairman had convinced the leadership to ask for Pastor Larry's resignation. With a small severance package and a promised recommendation, the pastor was removed. Oh, by the way, the congregation sat through the proceedings, well aware of the deacon's misconduct but unwilling to confront him.

Sad to say, this scenario is played out over and over. Members hunker down in church roles, living lives in direct contradiction to the tenets of Scripture with little regard for the reputation of the church. Some members are so openly hostile in their lifestyle that few pastors worth their salt (no pun intended) can in good conscience avoid the confrontation. The only problem is that the laity is so uncomfortable with confrontation that the matter falls almost completely on the shoulders of the senior pastor. Even staff, though supportive privately, may choose publicly to remain anonymous. Hey, they've got to make a living. The result is an ever-growing number of clergy who opt out of the disciplinary process altogether, frightened by the stories of men like Pastor Larry.

Some pastors, when questioned about confrontation, will try to justify their neutrality by responding with a statement such as, "I just preach the Word and let the Holy Spirit do the convicting." Though that sounds spiritual, ministers such as these have discovered the road of least resistance, making the life of fellow pastors who *do* address sin in the ranks more miserable and lonely. In fact, these I-just-preach-the-Word pastors remind me of parents who, though they may talk a good line, seldom follow up. Instead of enforcing some level of discipline, they allow their children to live in disobedience, thereby making the job of parents who do require adherence more difficult. Ministers like these tend to hide behind the pulpit, using a shotgun delivery that sprinkles a few pellets on the general assembly while never homing in on specific abuses in the congregation. Their delivery is nonthreatening, tickling the ears of congregants with a dusting of divinity, you might say. They have discovered who butters their bread, and they hold the slice up in the most nonthreatening way possible. They resemble a hireling who is willing to compromise the purity of the bride of Christ for comfort. They are like a father who admits that his daughter is going to be promiscuous, so he puts her on birth control.

They are nothing like the prophet Nathan, who wielded the sword of a prophetic word so close to David's throat after the king of Israel's rendezvous with Bathsheba that no answer could be given but "guilty."

They are under-shepherds who remain distant and aloof from their flock, allowing the assembly to live outside the parameters of God's law, threatening the Great Commission.

It is critical to the health of a church that the pastor, above all others, recognizes the damage of willful, defiant disobedience by members who chose to live their rebellion in the public arena. It is one thing for a child to be disobedient; it is quite another to do so publicly in plain sight of the parent and to the annoyance of others. For example, it is not a spoiled child who disrupts a restaurant as much as it is the parent's disregard of the child's behavior. Other patrons are not saying, "Why won't that child behave?" Rather, they are asking, "Why doesn't the parent do something about it?" The parent's failure or nonchalant attitude will cause the entire establishment to become angry, perhaps toward the child but most likely toward the oblivious parent.

The same is true of the public toward an apathetic church and its leadership. It is important to note that if a pastor is unconcerned about a member's conduct, the congregation will be as well. George Bernard Shaw said, "The worst sin is not to hate a fellow creature but to be indifferent toward him. That's the essence of humanity." If the pastor does not take sin seriously, then he need not expect the membership to be any different.

Added to this is the fact that if pastors begin to stand as Pastor Larry did, then we can expect a growing number of terminations. Something even more tragic and noted by many clergy is the reluctance on the part of their denominational leaders to stand with them. Many denominations are choosing to remain neutral on forced terminations rather than conducting investigations to determine if there is in fact a biblical principle being violated. Why? They perceive their role as one of peacemaking rather than determining what is right. (They also know where their funds are coming from.) I think it was Spurgeon who said, "Just because things are calm doesn't mean they're right." Some pastors govern their ministry by such.

The outcome of this is that denominations and ministers have discovered that silence is paramount to survival. They have learned how to lead and even preach in such a way that few, if any, are offended. They acquire a mode of sermon delivery that I earlier termed the "shotgun approach," which sprays the congregation with a generic, nonthreatening message. By *nonthreatening* I mean a sermon that does not call anyone's behavior into question. Speaking in generalities, they stroll through the Scriptures with a chorus of appreciative amens, armed with "how to" and "felt need." They learn to walk parishioners along the streets of Scripture, careful to avoid Sacrificial Strait, Repentance Road, or Abandonment Alley. For our cartoon friend who is living outside the box, there is little hope with a pastor such as this. Rather than warning him, his minister is humming a lullaby while he dozes in the pew.

If confrontation and discipline is the hope of the church, then it will most assuredly be paved with the blood of those who lead her. Pastors will be the point men in the battle. To shirk the responsibility and turn a deaf ear will come back to haunt him with an eternal sound. Hell is filled with the unconfronted, her corridors lined with unregenerate church members who may be anxiously awaiting the arrival of their leaders.

Again, forgive me for pounding a point, but a warning should be given to those denominational entities that sit on the sideline of the conflict and refuse to stand with clergy on clearly defined biblical issues. Sad to say, given time, they will see their empires crumble, just like denominations who choose to wallow in the mud of compromise and indifference. The decision to embrace a position of neutrality is done for one reason: funding. However, this action only serves to destroy the integrity of all involved. Such leaders fail to realize that local churches will eventually die and so will entire denominations.

How can the laity help the pastor? In the case of Pastor Larry, there is the very real danger that both church and the leader can feel lonely and bullied. To ensure that this is not a factor, sister churches and denominational structures should be involved in the process. For instance, when a leader takes a clear biblical stance, all others— pastors, laity, and denomination—should seek to align themselves with that person. If they choose not to do so, the clergy becomes a "lone ranger."

The autonomy of the local church is a poor excuse and is often a cover for a do-nothing attitude within both churches and denominational entities. Support of the leadership is not "choosing up sides" but rather a commitment to the tenets of Scripture. In other words, conflict is not to be based on the personalities involved, which is often the case, but rather on a clear teaching of Scripture. The hope of confrontation is to confront for the expressed purpose of repentance.

Often when a pastor or church leader has chosen to take a stand on a biblical issue, there can be a distancing by the congregation. By *distancing* I mean that there is a time in which the congregation pulls away from the leadership. Though they may recognize the moral and ethical rightness of a leader's stand, they are hesitant to get involved. Why? Well, let's face it; most churches are gripped by either a power-hungry minority or a let's-just-all-get-along-regardless group. Both of these act as a silencer on the barrel of confrontation.

A *power group* tends to see itself as a collection of the ones in charge, those who are responsible for maintaining the vision, order, and most of all, peace. So if the pastor takes a biblical stand on an issue that is detrimental to any of the above, the power group comes in to tell him to tone it down. They say, "We know you're right, but if you continue to address this, it will hurt our church." Note the word *our*. So the ultimatum is given: "Either drop it or leave." It is no longer about what the Bible may teach; it is more about what will protect the institution from any conflict—the point being that conflict is seen as something bad or unchristian. Of course, if conflict was always bad and something to be avoided, then every prophet and preacher, including Christ himself, was wrong. But we know this is not true. In fact, if anything, Paul created conflict for the sake of doctrinal integrity and personal holiness.

As a layperson, one must make every effort, once the biblical ramifications are deemed correct, to align themselves alongside the leadership. Again, this should only be done when the leadership stands in agreement to a scriptural mandate. How can someone do this? First, members can address the correct biblical view as applied to the issue—in private circles, friendships, and fellowships. Second, when given the opportunity, one can stand with the leadership in a business meeting and other public events. Third, when possible, one can remind the let's-just-all-get-along-regardless group that compromise of scriptural truth will be detrimental to the long-term health of the church.

Finally, do all of the above with grace. None of this should ever be done with a choose-up-sides mentality. Ultimately, most leaders who find themselves in this situation are not looking for laity to merely align themselves alongside them; rather, they look for men and women of God who have studied the Scripture and are committed to biblical accuracy and truth. Never forget that this difficult business of the church should be bathed in prayer.

One of the most challenging moments in my ministry came when I addressed the issue of race relations in the deep south. After scheduling a man of another race to speak, I discovered a large group of congregants who were not happy—38 percent, to be exact. Though I made attempts to sort out the problem, nothing short of asking the speaker not to come would suffice, which I could not do. This was one of the darkest chapters of my life, and though I was thankful for support, much of it came by those who loved me but may not have understood the biblical importance of what was at stake. If there is a danger in conflict, it is for the membership to divide based on personalities rather than biblical principle. If you choose to stand, it is paramount that you know why you are doing so. It cannot be merely because you like one person over another. Keep in mind that your power of persuasion as a leader or layperson rests in how well you know the subject up for debate. If you as a layperson are convinced, after research and study, that the leadership has taken a correct biblical stand, then you are under obligation to support them. This is not about personal preference but rather about what is biblically correct—and it should still be done with grace.

Let me warn that there are some subjects that the church has belabored for years and may never settle on this side of eternity. To divide a church over these issues is to do a disservice to the Great

Commission and the body of believers. The issue of race, however, is not one of these issues, and it left me with no alternative but to press forward. The man came and blessed our church, and yes, I was asked to leave. I ended up leaving the church and spending several years overseas, and ultimately I felt richly blessed for having done so. I have no regrets over my decision, and I still love those people to this day.

Before we leave this subject, there may be one last bit of counsel for those leaders who are still unconvinced and tend to maneuver clear of confrontation. George Barna discovered that leaders who are building dynamic, community-changing churches are quick to confront. He states:

> The leaders of stagnant churches rarely have a direct confrontation with people whose behavior or attitudes are both wrong and detrimental to the health of the body. Sometimes this is because the personality of the church leader is nonconfrontational. In other cases, it is because the dominant desire of church leaders is to keep people coming to church; confrontation, they reason, might diminish the body. In all cases, the refusal to confront that which is wrong or harmful is one manifestation of the inability of the church to model the principles that make the Scriptures so invaluable in a sinful world. User-friendly churches encountered their fair share of situations in which people needed to be confronted. These churches did not interpret *love* to mean "step over me if you must, but because I am Christian I will accept that abuse." Instead they took the "tough love" perspective: there is a distinction between right and wrong, and I will love you regardless, but I will also let you know when you are in the wrong. The confrontation had to be done delicately and in accordance with the guidelines provided in Scripture; but sin is not to be tolerated under any circumstances. (Barna, 2003, 111)

Some pastors and church leaders may find themselves uncomfortable with the last sentence: "Sin is not to be tolerated under any circumstances" (Barna, 2003, 111). Many feel that churches are called to accept people as they are, managing the masses without confronting patterns of sinful behavior. Yes, we must accept people as they are, yet to leave them in the condition in which we find them is to commit an injustice against the church, the community, and most of all to themselves. Why? Because, as Barna states, those "behaviors and attitudes are both wrong and detrimental to the health of the body" (Barna, 2003, 111). No body of believers can coexist with sin and not be affected. Pastors and denominational leaders must lead the way.

On a final note, let's consider Barna's words: "The refusal to confront that which is wrong or harmful is one manifestation of the inability of the church to model the principles that make the Scriptures so invaluable in a sinful world" (Barna, 2003, 111). Those outside the church need a pattern, a model they can follow in the home, in the work place, and with their friends. If the church and her leaders fail to model a biblical picture of confrontation and accountability, then the world will look elsewhere.

The woman at the beginning of this chapter was, sad to say, a bully. Her marriage, children, and friendships were in danger because of her abusive nature. I discovered as I spent time with her that any attempt on my part to address damaging personality traits were quickly smothered in anger or emotional meltdowns. Intimacy was lost because no one could confront her. Though she had come to me for help, every time I sought to address what was clearly a destructive trait, she would react. I thought, no wonder her husband wanted out.

With this in mind, let me add that for many relationships "fear governs communication." In other words, the possibility of confrontation is lost in the anxiety created when one party feels intimidated by the other. I have discovered that in most marriages, friendships, and other relationships there is one who will gravitate to the position of leadership; if he or she is not careful to wield authority with grace, intimacy will be lost.

Killing the Church

Lest I sound chauvinistic, I will say this. I have seen quiet, unassuming women who are married to strong, domineering men whose behavior is at times abrasive and hard, resulting in broken relationships. Though these women see the damage their husbands may be doing, they are reluctant to address it.

In President George W. Bush's memoirs, he shared a critical moment in his life when his wife, Laura, confronted him with a question that would change his life and set him on a path to the White House. He wrote, "It was a simple question. 'Can you remember the last day you didn't have a drink?' Laura asked in her calm, soothing voice. She wasn't threatening or nagging. She did expect an answer. My wife is the kind of person who picks her moments. This was one of them" (Bush, 2010, 1). He continued, "Quitting drinking was one of the toughest decisions I have ever made. Without it, none of the others that follow in this book would have been possible" (Bush, 2010, 3). His life—as well as a nation—was shaped for the better because someone invaded it with a question. A truth timely spoken would in time change him for the better. Thank you, Laura Bush.

A wife may see the damage caused by her husband continuing to live out a behavioral pattern that robs him—and her and their children and friendships—of true life-changing relationships. In fact, the only path toward healing and intimacy is for her fear to be faced and verbalized. When one person says to another, "I am afraid of you and your reaction, but I must tell you the truth because we cannot continue as we are now." People who love another person enough to say the above may be on the verge of real intimacy, even though the process may be stressful. Why? Fear can and often does jeopardize the deepest levels of affection. But in the words of Coach Wooden, "A leader filled with this kind of love [speaking of Paul's definition of love in 1 Corinthians 13] is a powerful force and has the potential for creating a forceful organization" (Wooden, 2005, 88).

CHAPTER 4

Confrontation: Who Cares?

I N THE POPULAR SITCOM *SEINFELD,* a conversation takes place between Elaine and her boyfriend. Elaine asks, "Do you believe in God?" "Yes," her boyfriend replies. Elaine asks, "Is it a problem that I am not religious?" "Not for me," her boyfriend answers. "How's that?" she asks. Her boyfriend says, "I'm not the one going to hell" (Preaching Today.com, 2003, 197–98). Wow! Talk about not caring.

My wife often accuses me of answering questions before she asks them. She says it's spooky. Yet I can't help but read your thoughts right now: *What if the person I am confronting does not care, or worse, simply drops out of church or a relationship altogether?* Many pastors and church leaders are convinced that most people who need to be confronted couldn't care less. A pastor said as much in an interview: "If I confront a rebellious member, he won't care. He'll just leave and go somewhere else." After thirty-plus years in the ministry, I understand exactly where he is coming from. My tendency was and is much like his: to simply avoid any form of confrontation. Why? Because people don't care or will just leave and think nothing of it.

I heard a couple who, when attempting to confront one another about damaging behavior, usually ended their argument with one threatening the other: "Well, maybe we should just get a divorce." *The threat of desertion is often the greatest deterrent to confrontation.* Read that last sentence again. As leaders and laity alike, we convince ourselves that to confront anyone is either a waste of time or, worse, will only aggravate the problem. Often in the case of pastors, we sense that members care little about their church affiliation and see church membership as irrelevant. When members are confronted, they simply leave or fall away from the church. The result is that we avoid confrontation because we think they don't care.

Wow! Does the apathy of a congregant toward their membership dismiss the church from acting in a responsible way? Let's face it: to confront anyone is to recognize that they may choose to leave the relationship. In other words, they may have no problem walking away. However, in the case of a church member, the decision to leave a church should be taught as a serious breach of relationship between the member and the larger body of believers—and, more so, to Christ. Leaders must preach and teach a clear understanding of church membership prior to initiating any form of confrontation. For example, premarital counseling is done in order to teach a young couple who are contemplating marriage the seriousness of the commitment they are about to make. With that in mind, imagine if we as church leaders handled new, incoming church members like a young couple wanting to get married? Perhaps members don't care because we have trained them not to. The apathy of laity can never excuse the leadership from sounding the alarm.

Dale Earnhardt Sr., also known as "The Intimidator," died in a crash. Yet when the autopsy was made available to the general public, we were informed that had he been wearing a HANS (Head and Neck Safety Device), he most likely would have survived the crash. In essence, Earnhardt had ignored a device that could have saved his life. Imagine if you had been on the track near Earnhardt's crew prior to the race and knew what was about to take place. How would you have addressed his apathy concerning a safety device? Just because a member doesn't care, doesn't mean leadership shouldn't. Pastors should so value church membership that they preach it with urgency, understanding that the safety of the individual member is strengthened by church affiliation. Perhaps we could say that the church is the "Head and *Heart* Safety Device." But with that said, sometimes all we do is not sufficient, and people are determined to leave. How are we to process this, and what should be our response when it occurs?

The apostle John, who lost large groups of members, gives us a clue as to why people leave. He reminded his congregation, "They left us, but they were never really with us. If they had been, they would have stuck it out with us, loyal to the end. In leaving, they showed their true colors, showed they never did belong" (1 John 2:19 The Message). In his comments on this passage, F. F. Bruce states, "The dissenters [who] had left the apostolic fellowship simply showed that at the heart they had never belonged to it … Continuance is the test of reality" (Bruce, 1970, 69).

If that is the case, then there are a lot of churches in trouble. Why? Because most congregations have evolved into a level of acceptance, believing that this is just the way it is. Few churches are willing to confront, because they don't think those who are being confronted will care anyway. Today, "no-shows" have become such a serious problem that the average church limps along so crippled they can hardly function. Most churches operate with half their membership and refuse to address the issues, fearful they may lose the other half. As one pastor said, "It is better to have them come on occasion than to not have them come at all." And yes, he went on to say what most pastors admit. "If I do confront them about their attendance—or for that matter, about any area of their lives—they will just leave and go somewhere else."

This is so alien to the words of the apostle John. Here is Gary M. Burge's commentary on 1 John 2:19: "'Their departure is evidence,' says John, 'that they were never a part of the church in the first place. Their falsehood has been unveiled'" (Burge, 1996, 127). In other words, the question of attendance is a clear indicator as to true membership—a membership not in an institution but rather in a body.

James Montgomery Boice expands the thought. "Being faced with a major defection in their ranks, the Christians of Asia Minor might be tempted to be discouraged, but now John adds that the defection has a good purpose. These 'went out' from us, he says, in order that it might show that none of them belonged to us. In other words, the defection has the effect of purifying the church and revealing both truth and error in true colors" (Boice, 1979, 86). Did you notice that Boice said that the defection has a good purpose? The defection more clearly defines who the real followers of Christ are.

I think the real danger is that we as leaders *do not allow the defection*. John did not run after those who were leaving, nor did he renegotiate the mission. He let them go. If they did not care, then it only defined more clearly what was in their hearts. So, back to my spooky intuition: what if the leadership will not allow the defection and instead hangs on to the stragglers? Think about that. What if the church takes on a passive role, whereby they allow individuals to remain in the membership without any accountability, because they think people don't care and no one wants to make the situation worse by confronting them? Remember this: people don't care because we have allowed them not to. For example, a parent tells a child to mow the grass, that if they do not do so there will be repercussions. The child responds, "I don't care," to which the parent answers, "I bet I can make you care." What the parent means here is that the child understands there is a cost to not caring.

Some might even argue, "So what? We are talking about people who are "members in name only." That is true, but the name is not yours; it is Jesus Christ's. Ultimately, it is his name that receives the bad press, and it is his mission that suffers.

"Mark Cuban, owner of the NBA's Dallas Mavericks, recently offered WGN Chicago Radio sports-talk host David Kaplan $50,000 to change his name legally to "Dallas Maverick." When Kaplan politely declined, Cuban sweetened the offer. Cuban would pay Kaplan $100,000 and donate $100,000 to Kaplan's favorite charity if he took the name for one year. After some soul-searching and being bombarded by e-mails from listeners who said he was crazy to turn down the money, Kaplan held firm and told Cuban no. Kaplan explained: "I'd be saying I'd do anything for money, and that bothers me. My name is my birthright. I'd like to preserve my integrity and credibility" (Preaching Today, 2003, 139).

Undoubtedly, there is a lot to a name. I am bothered by apathy toward the name *Christian*—and more so when one speaks about church membership as if it is no big deal. Today, many see church affiliation as nothing more than a tag, an identification that for all practical purposes means little and can be disposed of by simply ignoring it. Wrong! Membership is identity. Churches that choose to remain neutral on the subject of membership, ignoring the lifestyle of its members, sabotage their very mission. They also do so when they allow members to remain on the rolls with little or no concern as to their presence within the fellowship. As we saw a moment ago, John saw the absent members as making a clear statement that was not to be ignored by the leadership: "They left us, but they were never really with us" (1 John 2:19 The Message). No doubt, if this was communicated to the fellowship, it was also communicated to those individuals who had left.

Now, let's return to the subject of "not caring" evidenced in defection. Many leaders want to avoid the damage that occurs when a member is confronted, where a congregant gets mad and leaves. Yet the church of the twenty-first century must recognize what was no doubt clearly understood by the first-century congregation: if confrontation is enough to drive a member away, then perhaps they were never a member to begin with. Though members are by nature prone to wander, those members who wander and remain so may never have been a part of the church to begin with. If they don't care, then does that not speak to their spiritual condition? Tragically, many pastors, even in light of these passages, are still reluctant to address public, habitual disobedience. If pressed as to their fears, it is always the same: "I am afraid they will shrug their shoulders in indifference or, worse, answer with a defiant 'go ahead and take your best shot.'" How sad. Churches negate scriptural mandates because a member doesn't care or threatens with a reprisal of their own.

James gives good counsel without fear. "My brothers, if one of you should wander from the truth and someone should bring him back, remember this: Whoever turns a sinner from the error of his way will save him from death and cover over a multitude of sins" (James 5:19–20

NIV). Here the leader of the church at Jerusalem ends his letter with a call to confront and even warns his readers that they dare not shirk the responsibility. Why? Because he sees the danger that can ensue when disobedient lives are allowed to find their own way. Just because members do not care does not excuse the church from confronting. Today's non-response has threatened the mandate of the church perhaps more than any period of persecution. We don't have a "bully pulpit" but rather a "bully pew." The result has been apostasy of such proportions that turning the church around may cost more than many churches are willing to pay. Most leaders admit that it is not revival we need but rather repentance, their conviction being that the church is so contaminated that only radical surgery can save her at this point.

Yet many leaders wait on an act of God rather than a process initiated by the church and guided by the Scriptures. The primary avenue of correction throughout Scripture has always been the body of believers taking action upon themselves. John MacArthur states in his commentary on Matthew, chapters 16–23, "A Christian who is not deeply concerned about bringing a fellow Christian back from his sin needs spiritual help himself. Smug indifference, not to mention self-righteous contempt, has no part in the life of a spiritual Christian, nor do sentimentality or cowardice that hide behind a false humility. The spiritual Christian neither condemns nor justifies a sinning brother. His concern is for the holiness and blessing of the offending brother, the purity and integrity of the church, and the honor and glory of God" (MacArthur, 1988, 128).

In both the Old and New Testaments, people enforced Levitical law, and though some abused it, it was not abandoned. To shirk biblical responsibility because of the potential reaction of the guilty party is equivalent to a parent watching his child wander onto a busy street and saying, "I believe you should let them find their own way." Too many churches have taken this approach, dismissing any form of biblical confrontation, thereby endangering the lives of their members. Many today believe that the parishioner in question will simply respond, "I don't care," and the church answers, "If they don't care, why should I?"

Why take action to sever a relationship with a party who cares nothing about the relationship to begin with?

Just because a church member does not care about their standing doesn't mean that the church is excused from taking action. The church at Corinth tried to do something very similar when they ignored an incestuous relationship within the membership, and Paul rebuked them for their do-nothing attitude in this case. A member of the Corinthian congregation had been, as my grandmother use to say, "shacking up" with a woman who was his stepmother. So Paul's response was, "It is actually reported that there is immorality among you, and immorality of such a kind as does not exist even among the Gentiles, that someone has his father's wife. You have become arrogant and have not mourned instead, so that the one who had done this deed would be removed from your midst. For I, on my part, though absent in body but present in spirit, have already judged him" (1 Corinthians 5:1–3 NASV). How the man might respond was not a factor.

John MacArthur comments, "This chapter is not directed at the believers, or 'so called' believers (v. 11), who were committing the sins but at the rest of the church who stood by doing nothing about it." He goes on to say, "Paul's first step was to show them that the immorality was immorality and that it was serious and should not be tolerated—something they already should have known" (MacArthur, 1988, 128). Gordon H. Clark goes further, stating, "*Complacent* is really too weak a word. The Corinthians actually congratulated themselves on being so broad-minded" (Clark, 1975, 79).

In *Effective Body Building*, C. Peter Wagner agrees. "They were not boasting that they had a case of incest. Rather, their pride may well have been centered in their concept of ethical broad-mindedness. The elders may have said to one another as they discussed the case: 'What our good brother does in his private life is entirely his business'" (Wagner, 1982, 58). Paul knew that if Corinth continued to neglect their responsibility, the result could be his own intervention or, worse, God's. This brings up the question: is it possible that some of our sicknesses and even untimely deaths could be attributed to the unwillingness of the membership to address habitual disobedience? We will investigate this further in the next chapter. Without a clear understanding by new converts as to the critical importance of church membership, the prospects of "fixing church discipline" are remote.

Helping the Laity: Confronting the Indifferent

There have been those moments in marriage counseling when one of the parties being counseled simply got up and left. In the middle of gut-wrenching honesty and great strides, a husband or wife has just stood up and said, "I've had enough of this," and walked out. I have seen counseling progressing in a session, when at a critical moment, one member gets mad and leaves. When this happens, almost without exception, the one left sitting there will look at me and say, "I knew that was coming." Then the individual usually goes on to say that the spouse doesn't care. At this point, the one still seated is questioning the value of the session and, more so, the confrontation itself. Often one party is convinced that the other party does not care, so he or she cowers down, refusing to confront, believing that the other side will simply abandon the relationship altogether. Yet the truth is that some relationships need to be put at risk. In other words, take the chance.

Think about it. Have you ever noticed someone who grates on everyone's nerves? No matter how hard he tries to get along with others, no one wants to be around him. And to make matters worse, though you may be the closest thing he has to a friend, you have avoided the issue. When he's asked for your insight as to why this happens, you've responded—no, you've *lied*—and said, "I don't know." In other words, you were willing to allow a friend to continue in superficial relationships rather than tell him the truth. In fact, here's the big question: "Would you be willing to lose a friend in order to make them aware of a flaw in their personality, a personality quirk that is robbing them of any real, lasting relationships?"

This chapter began with the title "Who Cares?", meaning that the average church member doesn't value his church membership or church/parishioner relationship enough to care, even if he were to be confronted. But the more critical issue is this: do you value a spouse or a friend enough to confront them with a painful truth? Are you willing to love a person enough to tell him something that would improve the quality of his life? Would you be willing to confront, even if it meant that this person would walk away from the relationship? Sad to say, most of our acquaintances are built on dishonesty rather than honesty, the dishonesty being that we would rather be *liked* than *truthful*. Are you willing to say good-bye to a relationship for the sake of truth? Please read that question again.

Michael Oher, the true-life star of the hit movie *The Blind Side*, said in his biography, "If you make a decision, its never too late to make the right one … I will always love my family—my siblings and my mother—and we have been through a whole lot together. But that doesn't mean that I need to keep negative people in my life. My biological mother has shown me time and again through her poor decisions that she values certain things more than she values her relationship with her children. I've tried to put her in rehab, I've tried to help her however I could, but I have finally realized the sad truth—that she and I really don't have a relationship anymore" (Oher, 2010, 182). These words from a man who was once a homeless kid wandering the streets of Memphis—one who would, through a course of events, become a national figure—are also true of the church. Leaders must recognize that, regardless of their efforts, some people will not be recovered, and Oher's words may be the final diagnosis: "I have realized the sad truth—that she and I really don't have a relationship anymore."

But let's not end on a negative note. Instead, let me share a better hope.

A Story of Confrontation

Several years ago, I attended a baseball game where a pastor friend was coaching. In the course of a tightly contested match, the third-base umpire made a questionable call. My friend, who is known as a strong competitor, exploded out of the dugout and launched into a verbal showdown. In moments, the scene escalated into parents and players becoming involved. Knowing that the situation was getting out of hand, I slipped down to the field close to the fence and called him to the side. My warning was simple: "Your testimony is about to be damaged if you don't drop it."

I can still see his expression as he looked up at the stands and then at his players. He realized that this little ball-field congregation was no longer watching a coach but rather a local pastor. He whispered a thank-you, apologized to the base umpire and then to the crowd, and then sat down in the dugout. Now the truth is, I could have just sat back and watched while a friend not only blew his testimony but also that of his church. Was it easy to approach him? No. In fact, I must admit there was even a measure of fear. The confrontation was gentle but firm, being careful not to draw any more attention then was necessary.

This is an important part of confronting professing Christians in public disobedience. *When correction becomes as volatile as the infraction itself, I must reconsider whether I am the right person to proceed.* Another thing to remember is that timing is critical. In this case, it was appropriate for the moment, but in other cases, it might not have been. Public correction will usually backfire if the one being corrected feels embarrassed or isolated. Notice that in this case, I came to where my friend was and whispered in such a way as to not be heard by those close by.

I believe that the workplace rather than a ball field will probably be the front line for many in this battle. For instance, inappropriate language, crude jesting, flirtation, or even adultery, though the accepted norm in the working world, are not to be tolerated in the lives of believers. Christians who live out testimonies that are contrary to the faith they hold—in the office or on a ball field—can cost the church. However, let me say again that the *way* a fellow believer is addressed will, for all practical purposes, determine if there is further damage or not. Anything less than a biblical approach will only serve to alienate the member further—perhaps forever. In fact, if an individual is mishandled, male or female, the result is usually an alliance of the "disenchanted." In other words, you will have a *group* at the work place that has banded together in accusing "The Church"—and you—of being harsh and judgmental. Nonetheless, one must remember that a certain amount of this will happen anyway because of those who have no intentions toward Christlikeness.

CHAPTER 5

Failure to Confront: Cost to the Person

THE JUDGE PEERED OVER THE top of his glasses at the teenager and his father. The boy, who had been involved in one petty act of vandalism after another, stood with a slight smirk on his face. Annoyed at the arrogance, the judge turned to the father with this warning: "Sir, either you get control of your son, or one day soon, I will." The admonition was clear. Unless the father was able to change the behavior of his son, the judge would see him again, and this time the kid would feel the full weight of the law.

Now, with that in mind, is it possible that God says much the same to the church? *Either you get control of your member or I will.* The principle is that when a lower authority fails to control the actions of those for whom they are accountable, then a higher authority must intervene. Paul said as much when he warned the church at Corinth, "A man ought to examine himself before he eats of the bread and drinks of the cup. For anyone who eats and drinks without recognizing the body of the Lord eats and drinks judgment on himself" (1 Corinthians 11:28–30 NIV). In this case, Paul spoke of the lower authority as individual members who were to examine their own lives to determine if they were living within the dictates of Scripture before taking communion. Paul saw that a member who refused to exercise this responsibility himself was in danger of a higher authority's action—either the church or, in this case, God.

Let me illustrate. Recently during a communion service, the chairman of our deacon body, though serving the sacraments to others, refused them for himself. Afterward, he mentioned to me the passage in 1 Corinthians and his feelings of unworthiness at the time. He confided that his life was not where it needed to be. In relation to our father-and-son illustration above, this would be the equivalent of the son taking responsibility for his actions without the judge or the father having to intervene.

I understood the deacon, for it hadn't been that long ago that I had done the same thing. After a terrible week—one in which I felt my behavior had been less than Christlike—I felt ill-equipped to preach. So, with that weighing on me, I had walked to the pulpit, opened my Bible, and begun to read out of Luke. At times I wept along with the congregation. Like my deacon, I had exercised authority over my life without the intervention of anyone. Had I not done so and chosen instead to preach the message I had worked on, I do believe there would have been repercussions. The deacon admitted much the same by his own decision to refuse the sacraments.

The congregation at Corinth had suffered more than her share of sickness and deaths. Consequently, Paul didn't mince words, suggesting that the physical maladies might be evidence of the higher authority's (God's) intervention. "For anyone who eats and drinks without recognizing the body of the Lord eats and drinks judgment on himself. That is why many among you are weak and sick, and a number of you have fallen asleep. But if we judged ourselves, we would not come under judgment" (1 Corinthians 11:29–31 NIV). Note the words: *but if we judged ourselves, we would not come under judgment.* Think on the depth of that statement for a moment. Let's make this personal. Could it be that some of the heartache and difficulties that come into our lives are the result of disobedience? Is it possible that even problems with health, finances, and so on are the result of sin or negligence to scriptural mandates? Does God bring a measure of discipline into our lives because we fail to do so? Do we know ourselves as well as we think we do?

Drew Brees, the quarterback of the New Orleans Saints, tells of his early years as an NFL quarterback and the quest to hang on to his position, which at that time was with the San Diego Chargers. Tom House, a pitching coach with USC who held a doctorate in psychology, agreed to help Drew Brees. Drew states, "Finally, Tom suggested I do what he called a 'star profile,' which is basically a personality test tweaked for athletes. The questions reveal a lot about what makes you tick as an athlete and a person and the way you approach life—and where you might need some improvement. I saw myself as an outgoing, assertive person. The profile revealed the opposite. So my first task was to get my perception in line with reality, to learn the truth about myself." Wow! How many of us have no grasp of who we really are, often going through life with a false perception and never coming to a knowledge of the truth—the truth about ourselves? (Fabry, 2010, 64).

Does God bring a measure of discipline into our lives because we don't know who we are? Do we fail to confront ourselves or allow others to do so? Could it be that some members suffer under the hand of God because the church has failed to exercise her jurisdiction over those entrusted to her care? The church is called to maintain control over the membership, much like the father was called to maintain control over the behavior of his son. If church or father fail, then the higher authority will step in. Again, to belabor the point: if either church or father relinquishes this parental right, then the higher authority will get involved.

Like the judge at the beginning of this chapter, God requires accountability by those in positions of leadership; in other words, ministers have a parental role much like the father of the teenager. The judge held the father responsible, just as God holds the church responsible for the actions of her members. And if God has to step in and take over the disciplinary process, the intervention will carry a much stiffer sentence. In the case of the church at Corinth, the stiffer sentence was sickness and death. Paul was adamant with the leaders at Corinth, telling them that because they had failed to confront and control their members, they had left God with no alternative but to step in and discipline the membership himself.

Perhaps it would be good to note that as long as the leaders and members are involved in confrontation and discipline, God may hold back his own intervention. In the opening story, the judge allowed the father to get control of the son first. In essence, he showed mercy to the son by refusing to enforce the judicial process. The judge was willing to wait and see if the dad could bring the destructive behavior in line. By this, the judge was saying that he preferred not to be involved, in hopes that the milder form of confrontation would suffice.

I believe there is a principle here: churches and leaders who fail to confront endanger their congregations. If the father in the illustration ignores the judge's warning, he puts his son's life in the cross hairs of the judge's wrath. Tragically, the situation moves from a teenager being sent to his room or losing the car keys to incarceration. Keep in mind that a higher authority can and usually will relinquish or hold off intervention when a lower authority is dealing with the matter.

I think it is important to note that if the father of the rebellious son casually dismisses the act as just normal adolescent ramblings, then the judge now has a problem with the father. With this in mind, the same could be said of God, who has a problem with any church that overlooks the unbiblical behavior of its members. Why is that so? Because we now have a crisis that requires *both* parties to be confronted and disciplined. For example, suppose you own a china shop, and a mother with a defiant, rambunctious child enters. The child, wrestling and rough-housing, breaks a costly piece of porcelain. Who will pay? You guessed it: the parent. Why? Because the parent is the authority in charge. In fact, the owner of the shop would have little respect for someone who knowingly allowed the rebellion.

In the passage in 1 Corinthians, Paul, with apostolic authority, admits that these illnesses and even deaths were due to the Corinthian members' failure to grasp the depth of the meaning behind the Lord's Supper. In fact, Paul uses the verb *paideuomai* to indicate the way a parent disciplines to correct a wayward child. Barclay states, "These misfortunes are not sent to destroy them but to discipline them and to bring them back to the right way" (Barclay 1954, 117). What is so tragic is that much, if not all, of this heartache could have been avoided if only the body of believers would have addressed these patterns of disobedience early on. Read that last sentence again. John MacArthur expands this thought by stating, "God sends individual chastening to push offenders back toward righteous behavior, and sends death to some in the church to encourage those who remain to choose holiness rather than sin" (MacArthur, 1984, 128).

I like MacArthur's wording: "to push offenders back toward righteous living." It reminds me of a story I heard years ago about a little boy who was standing at the edge of a lake, crying. A businessman came along and recognized that the lad's boat had drifted too far out. So he took off his jacket, gathered a handful of rocks, and tossed one after another on the far side of the vessel. The waves created soon moved the child's toy back into his possession. Although the boy could not understand the man's actions in the beginning, he did understand in time. Why? Because his boat was moving closer to the shore and coming back into his hands.

Sometimes the church is called upon to create a disturbance in the life of a professing believer to bring him back to the fellowship. This disturbance usually comes in the form of confrontation, which is done to correct behavior that is contrary to the mission of the church. Critical to the well-being of the church are leaders who recognize that the membership must not be left alone when drifting. This is the same counsel we give to parents who are tempted to let their children raise themselves, the danger being that behavioral patterns of disobedience will develop when children or members are left to themselves.

Perhaps this is a good place to stop and warn pastors once again. Ministers who are tempted to cushion the membership rolls at the expense of the integrity of the church are guilty of high treason in the army of God. What may be even worse is the endangering of the very lives of those who make up the body of believers.

The bottom line is clear. Failure by any church to confront its membership puts the matter in the hands of God and thereby jeopardizes the health and well-being of all its members. William G. Blaikie says that within the "solidarity of man … in families, we suffer for one another's faults, even when we hold them in abhorrence. We benefit by one another's virtues, though we may have done our utmost to discourage and destroy them" (Blaikie, 1893, 172–73). In other words, we are a corporate body, not only as families but also as communities—and ultimately as a body of believers, the body of Christ.

Helping the Laity: The Danger of Nonconfrontation

Taking this to the realm of individual relationships is to recognize that just as the church may be liable to God for poor supervision, so are we when we choose to ignore disobedience. Far too many believers are silent in friendships when a "timely word" might save much heartache. To ignore anyone who has moved "outside the box" may, in fact, be jeopardizing his or her life. Just as the church must exercise her authority over each member, so must individual believers do the same in their relationships—marriage, parenting, and friendships.

For example, you have a friend who has developed a relationship with a work associate that appears to be much too intimate for one who is married. Instead of intervening, you keep quiet. You become convinced that it is not your place to confront, while at the same time your friend moves closer and closer to a disaster. In other words, a crisis is developing while you lie low. Keep in mind that, as we saw a moment ago, your decision to remain neutral is to turn your friend over to a higher authority, and in the case of a believer, that higher authority is God. And let's face it: once God steps in, the dynamics of discipline change drastically. Wow! You had the potential for saving your friend much heartache but chose not to. Why? Because you valued their approval over what was right.

Let's take a moment and remind ourselves that we could stop a lot of bad "crops" if we would just get in the way of the one doing the sowing. A friend is slinging "weed seed," and all we can do is shake our head and gossip at the water fountain, because we want to be liked rather than right. We long for acceptance by our friends to the degree that we thumb our nose at God and mutter, "It's his problem, not mine." Do we value temporal, immediate fellowship with someone more than we care about their long-term health and happiness? Has it ever occurred to you that one day, somewhere down the road, a friend may show up on your doorstep and say, "Thank you for being straight"? Have you ever thought about heaven and imagined someone coming up to you and telling you that your honesty, though it hurt at the time, saved them from a multitude of mistakes? No wonder James 5:19–20 speaks so clearly to those who risk friendships to turn a person away from sin. Relationships that are real will, in the end, survive *truthful exchanges.*

Richard Carlson, author of *Don't Sweat the Small Stuff,* says he was concerned when he heard that Monica Lewinsky's father said he hadn't talked to her about her alleged involvement with President Clinton. Carlson concluded from this, "When people love each other, they share what's going on in their lives. It's okay to be honest, even if that honesty proves you're in trouble or made a mistake" (May, 2000, 263).

Think about Carlson's statement. The trouble in the case of Lewinsky may have been a long time in coming due to the lack of communication between father and daughter. Further, the father's reluctance to approach his daughter about her life contributed not only to her demise but to that of a president as well. Wow. Dad had lived his entire life avoiding any form of confrontation with his daughter. Sometimes we parents so long for acceptance in our relationships with our children that we are unwilling to risk honesty and truth. If this was the pattern of Monica Lewinsky's father, then it is understandable why she ended up in this crisis. As authority figures—parents or pastors—there is continual temptation to avoid difficult subjects. We can so desire favor that we are willing to overlook the poor life choices of those closest to us—choices that, if lived out, will lead to catastrophic mistakes.

"On May 28, 1972, the Duke of Windsor, the uncrowned King Edward VIII, died in Paris. On the same evening, a television program recounted the main events of his life. Viewers watched film footage in which the duke answered questions about his upbringing, his brief reign, and his eventual abdication. Recalling his boyhood as Prince of

Wales, he said: 'My father (King George V) was a strict disciplinarian. Sometimes when I had done something wrong, he would admonish me, saying, "My dear boy, you must always remember who you are"'" (Larson and Zahn, 2002, 133). Confrontation in the case of a Christian may be as simple as reminding someone of who they are. This is not just a matter of the name we bear but of the position we hold, those whom we represent, and the damage done when we fail.

CHAPTER 6

Failure to Confront: Cost to the Church

I N HIS BOOK, *THROUGH MY EYES*, Tim Tebow tells a story of confronting another player who was also a believer.

> I was two things to this team: a leader and a Christian. As a leader, I needed to be in front and set an example. As a Christian, I needed to lead in a manner that was pleasing to Christ. This ethic can lead to conflict, if those around me do not agree. A good example of this conflict came when I was a freshman. The team was running the stadium steps one morning around six o'clock. We always began our workout when it was dark in the Swamp. I was determined to finish first; however, to make it more meaningful, I wanted to start in the back. As I would pass each player going up the stadium steps, I would encourage them to push harder. One teammate was offended by my comments. He gave me a real bad look and said he was doing what he thought was right. I kept going and finished a long time before he did.
>
> In the locker room, and well after everyone else had gone, I asked why he was not running any harder. To my surprise, he used God in his explanation. He said, "God told me this morning to stay back and run with the guy because I needed to encourage him." To be honest, I was

livid. Here was a very talented athlete, a team leader, and an outspoken Christian believing God wanted him to be a bad example to the team. You can see the conflict in our thinking.

I may have overstepped, but as a leader and fellow Christian, I felt I needed to confront him. I told him that he was extremely lazy and was inappropriately using God as an excuse. "If you want to bring God and spirituality into this, then you need to obey the authorities that God has put into your life. Coach Mike and Coach Meyer are your authorities, and to not work hard after they specifically told everyone to do so, and called out about your low effort, is wrong. Because they told you that, it is not acceptable to say that God told you to stay back and run with someone to influence or encourage him."

After pausing to let all this sink in, I added, "Maybe if you ran harder, you would influence that person to run harder himself. You are not being a good leader to anyone by being lazy, and using God as an excuse is unacceptable. (Tebow and Whitaker, 2011, 173–174)

The church, like the Florida Gators, is a team, with each member critical to the success of the others. The level of commitment by each individual member will either help or hinder the overall success of the mission. Let me illustrate with an Old Testament story where everyone suffered due to the indiscretion of one man.

The exodus of the Israelites from Egypt had begun under Moses' leadership and now continued under Joshua. Israel was riding a "high," leaving Jericho like a ball team after a Friday night victory, looking to their next opponent with the taste of triumph on their palate. The leadership—in this case, Joshua—knew that Ai, the next city in the campaign to take back the Promised Land, would be a minor skirmish compared to Jericho—an easy out, a stroll in the park, in essence, not requiring the first string. "Bring in the benchwarmers" was no doubt his comment to his commanders. Let them feel the bruise of battle, if in fact Ai could be considered a battle.

From the beginning of their exodus and throughout the taking of Jericho, Israel had been warned, "Don't take anything for yourselves. Defeat Jericho, take no prisoners, and above all else, take no pillage." Every Hebrew soldier knew that to disobey the edict would bring disaster on the nation—except one. "Surely no one would miss a couple of mementos from the battle," Achan reasoned to himself. So while the others gathered up their weapons, Achan slipped a few souvenirs into his pack. God wouldn't mind a small amount of insurrection. A robe from Babylonia, two hundred shekels of silver, and a wedge of gold would make little difference to the overall outcome of the military campaign.

Meanwhile, Joshua, oblivious to the criminal act of Achan and convinced by all the scouting reports that Ai would be a slaughter, continued his conquest. After a rousing speech, Joshua gave a few parting words, slipped into his tent, and waited to tally the results. However, that was not to be the case. Soon casualties were pouring in, and whatever crest they had been riding in the past was now painfully over. Fear gripped the camp. The entire operation stood in jeopardy. Joshua's approval ratings plummeted. Broken and desperate, the man who had once shadowed Moses was now collapsing to his knees, aware that his commander in chief, Jehovah, had not been at the battle.

Let's pick up the story in Joshua 7. "Then Joshua tore his clothes and fell facedown to the ground before the ark of the Lord, remaining there till evening. The elders of Israel did the same and sprinkled dust on their heads. And Joshua said, 'Sovereign Lord, why did you ever bring this people across the Jordan to deliver us into the hands of the Amorites to destroy us? If only we had been content to stay on the other side of the Jordan!'" (Joshua 7:6–7 NIV).

Wow! Imagine if the average congregation were to respond to failure in this fashion. What could God do? However, Israel didn't need to hold a prayer meeting; they needed repentance.

Skip to verses 10–11: "The Lord said to Joshua, 'Stand up! What are you doing down on your face? Israel has sinned; they have violated my covenant, which I commanded them to keep.

They have taken some of the devoted things; they have stolen, they have lied, they have put them with their own possessions."

Now wait a minute. God is omniscient, all-knowing. Surely he knew that the culprit, Achan, was the only one who had in fact disobeyed. You mean to tell me that God would jeopardize the whole crusade because of one man's sin? Why allow the death of an entire regiment of innocent soldiers just doing their job? The answer is that God was reminding Israel, and eventually the church, that we are a corporate body, each intricately tied to the other and ultimately to God. Joshua was about to discover that the culprit was not God or timing or poor leadership but rather disobedience by one man, Achan.

E. John Hamlin in his commentary, *Inheriting the Land*, states, "Because of one man's sin, a whole people could not stand before their enemies" (Hamlin, 1983, 58). Likewise, it is safe to say that a church with habitual disobedience in her ranks cannot stand before her enemies either. That statement right there should be enough to cause every pastor to reevaluate his apathy toward disobedience.

Now, returning to the passage, look at the inclusive language God uses in verses 11–12: "*Israel* has sinned; *they* have violated my covenant, which I commanded *them* to keep. *They* have taken some of the devoted things; *they* have lied, *they* have put them with their own possessions. That is why the *Israelites* cannot stand against *their* enemies; *they* turn their backs and run because *they* have been made liable to destruction. I will not be with *you* anymore unless *you* destroy whatever among *you* is devoted to destruction" (Joshua 7:10–11 NIV, emphasis mine).

Each italicized word demonstrates corporate responsibility, which in time will require corporate accountability. But even deeper is a principle relevant to both the nation of Israel and the church: God holds the body liable for the disobedience of an individual member. Why? Perhaps He is teaching a truth relevant to the future church: an individual sin that is not confessed or repented of affects us all." This tenet of Scripture reflects on the cancerous nature of habitual and undisciplined sin.

Take time to consume and digest this paragraph again. This is a truth tragically overlooked by the church and her leaders. In the case of Israel, God demanded holiness, and holiness could never be achieved without confrontation and discipline. So God forced the issue, pulling Achan's disobedience out into the open to stress the need for purity. Why?

Manford George Gutzke gives us a clue in his comments on this passage. "If one person sins, everybody suffers. It is much like saying that a chain is no stronger than its weakest link. If you try to pull something out with a chain, not every link has to break: the chain is broken when the weakest link in the chain breaks" (Gutzke, 1988, 20–21). Tim Tebow recognized this in a player, and so should the church in her members. Again, if one person sins, everybody suffers. Perhaps it is like a mother who walks into a messy kitchen, looks at all within earshot, and screams, "I want all of you to clean this mess up right now," only to hear one squeaky little voice respond, "But I didn't do it." To this, the mom counters, "I don't care who did it. Just get busy and clean it up!"

Returning to the passage at the beginning of the chapter, we find Israel in much the same predicament as the church at Corinth, experiencing a form of corporate responsibility. God is holding out on a single victory as well as the conquest of the Promised Land because of one man's sin!

With this in mind, I am convinced that no church can enjoy all that God may have for them as long as there is habitual, willful, public disobedience. Given enough time, everyone will be affected by the sinful behavior of one member. We are a *body* of believers.

Look at it this way. A criminal cannot sit in a courtroom and accuse his right hand of being the culprit merely because it held the gun. Imagine a convict claiming his hand was acting independently of his body. No judge would allow legal representation to suggest that one's extremity be reprimanded while sparing the rest of the body.

Paul stressed as much in his first letter to Corinth when he counseled the church to understand that they were a body of believers. If one member sinned, then the repercussions would be felt through the whole body. Each individual member has been placed by God to accomplish the task it has been designed to do. "The body is a unit, though it is made up of many parts; and though all its parts are many, they form one body. So it is with Christ. For we were all baptized by one Spirit into one body—whether Jews or Greeks, slave or free—and we were all given one Spirit to drink" (1 Corinthians 12:12–13 NIV). Remember that the man at Corinth who was "shacking up" was still considered by Paul to be a part of the body. If only churches and individual members could grasp that their behavior ultimately and eternally affects all who call themselves Christian.

I believe the Jewish people knew this and were holding to its principle in the most tragic chapter of their existence. Consider their encounter with Pilate over the conviction of Jesus Christ during his trial. "'What shall I do, then, with Jesus who is called Christ?' Pilate asked. They all answered, 'Crucify him!' 'Why? What crime has he committed?' asked Pilate. But they shouted all the louder, 'Crucify him!' When Pilate saw that he was getting nowhere, but that instead an uproar was starting, he took water and washed his hands in front of the crowd. 'I am innocent of this man's blood,' he said. 'It is your responsibility!' All the people answered, 'Let his blood be on *us* and *our* children'" (Matthew 27:22–25 NIV, emphasis mine).

The irony is that the nation of Israel understood at Calvary what many of today's churches are oblivious to. Sin in the corporate body, lived out in the public arena with no regard to correction or confrontation, will in the end bring judgment to all. (One might do well to read that last sentence aloud in the next church service.) The failure of any generation within the church to maintain their purity will create consequences to be reaped by generations yet to be born. If the church does not confront and seek to correct, then sin has a tendency to take on the character of a cancerous tumor, infecting the entire body. Keep in mind that the body of believers is joined across time. By this we cannot separate one generation from another. Christians in one generation have the potential to move the next generation of believers toward good or evil. If they neglect confrontation and allow their members to live oblivious to the tenets of Scripture, then they infect those yet to be born.

Taking this a step further, churches must be reminded we are not a headless monstrosity but rather a body whose head is none other than Christ himself. Every appendage is directly and intimately tied to the Son of God. Our conduct is a reflection not *of* Christ but rather *on* Christ. A manifestation poorly lived out causes a lost world to diminish the worth and dignity of her founder. No wonder the church has become the brunt of jokes and sarcasm. Her purity has been compromised, with little if any attempt to correct it. Her victories have been lost in corruption. We look like a parent who has a daughter in prostitution and a son in prison who is seeking to give advice and counsel on how to raise well-adjusted children. No parent is going to listen.

So is it any wonder that much of the nation—if not the world—is beginning to turn a deaf ear to the church? When the church returns to a high level of accountability for her own constituents, she will once again find a lost world that is willing to listen. In the illustration about a criminal who seeks to blame his hand rather than the rest of his body, the offender is going to be laughed out of court. The judge no doubt will remind him that his hand was cooperating with the rest of his body, and that includes the mind. As my second-grade teacher use to say, "Put on your thinking caps." The "head" is getting a bad rap for the behavior of its members.

A while back, I walked into my youngest son's room and tossed him a book of short excerpts from the biographies of great preachers and the movement of God that surrounded them. I encouraged him to look closely at the manifestations of the Spirit and ask, "Is God moving in our land or in our lives as he did in theirs?" I reminded him that every great movement of God has been prompted by a strong, corporate call to repentance. The cry of John the Baptist was a message of repentance, because Israel as a nation needed to repent of her apathy and indifference to sin.

Perhaps we can close this chapter by saying what God was trying to say to Joshua: *Son, Israel doesn't need a prayer meeting; she needs repentance.*

Joshua 7:10–11 says, "The Lord said to Joshua, 'Stand up! What are you doing on your face? Israel has sinned; they have violated my covenant, which I commanded them to keep. They have taken some of the devoted things, they have stolen, they have lied, they have put them with some of their own possessions.'" (Joshua 7:10–11 NIV).

Helping the Laity: The Failure to Confront Affects Us All

There is danger in thinking that another person's sin does not affect me. We tend to view other people's lives as independent of our own. *It's none of my business. It's not my problem.* That's probably what Adam and Eve thought. Our enemy the Devil would love to convince us all not to think, to quietly accept things the way they are. "How fortunate for leaders," Hitler said to his inner circle, "that men do not think. Make the lie big, make it simple, keep saying it, and eventually they will believe it" (Andrews, 2011, 32). But the truth is that sin always has far-reaching consequences that ultimately affect all mankind. We are eternally influenced by the good or bad choices that people make.

Recently, I was watching a reality show in which men and women were competing with unusual talents. One man's talent—if we can call it that—was to take dominoes and place them next to one another in row after row for what looked to be several yards. He had little tricks and gadgets nestled within each row, each of which was triggered by the fall of a single domino. On this particular night, he gave a nudge to the first domino and so began the show—until a groan came from the audience. You guessed it. One domino had failed to fall over another and so ended his production. Each domino was dependent upon the one before and after it to carry out its purpose. The failure of a single domino resulted in the entire performance being sabotaged.

Is this not reflective of the church and the role of each member? Like links in a chain or dominoes in a line, are we not dependent upon one another? The failure of any one believer can result in the failure of us all. Further, we must be reminded of the far-reaching impact of our lives on others when we get caught up in willful disobedience.

Killing the Church

Years ago I heard an old preacher say, "Sin will take you farther than you want to go, keep you longer than you want to stay, and cost you more than you want to pay." Though the statement is true, I would change "you" to "us." *Your* sin or *my* sin will take *us* farther than we want to go, keep *us* longer than we want to stay, and cost *us* more than we want to pay.

With that in mind, let me ask you a question. Would you intervene in someone's life if you knew that their sin was going to harm you and those you love personally? Please read that question again. I think I know the answer: *yes.* The tragedy is that every sin affects all of us. Is this not just one more reason to get involved in the lives of others? Again, Adam never thought about the implications of his and Eve's garden conspiracy on those yet to be born. So it is safe to say that any time we intervene in the life of another and confront them about an area of disobedience, we are saving others and ourselves from much heartache. We cannot allow our enemy to dupe us and those we lead into believing that sin is a private and personal matter.

In the classic Christmas movie, *It's a Wonderful Life,* George Bailey, troubled by life, makes the comment that he wishes he had never been born. In response, Clarence, an angel yet to earn his wings, is dispatched by God to give George a glimpse of a world without George. Over the course of the movie, our star, played by Jimmy Stewart, comes to the conclusion that his life has been influential in nearly every area of existence. The town, his family, friends, and even the world had been forever shaped by his life and the decisions he'd made. Though this was a movie, the truth is that everyone's life and how they live it affect us all. Perhaps the old statement, "No man is an island," is true. If any of us could choose to live our lives without confrontation—at the same time knowing that our choices carry consequences both here and in eternity—we would do humanity a great disservice by refusing to be confronted or to confront.

We dare not, for the sake of comfort or convenience, steer clear of involvement in the lives of others, especially when they are living in direct disobedience to the Word of God. What a lesson we could learn if an angel were to take us on a journey and show us the life of a poor decision; we would see the high cost of neglecting to confront.

George Bailey would learn that his decision to stay home and take over the family business was a choice that ultimately affected the lives of many—and even saved the lives of some. The attempt to confront, though it risks a friendship, may be our greatest act of service to humanity. Think that over for a moment before you move on. Who is God bringing to mind right now that is flirting with disaster? What dear friend do you have access to who may be making poor choices, choices that given time will result in much heartache to so many? Keep in mind that this is not the sole responsibility of the pastor, nor is it right to hope that some random, generic sermon will somehow spark a note of conviction in a friend's life. No, the truth is that God may be calling you to confront. But remember that this is not a witch-hunt; God has not called us to police the masses. In fact, Jesus used a parable to say as much. In the parable of the wheat and tares, he warned against a mindset where a person ventures out into the field, ripping and tearing out perceived tares, oblivious to the high cost of mistaken identity.

CHAPTER 7

Confrontation and Criticism

D O YOU WORRY ABOUT WHAT people think? Do you fret to the point that you're unable to approach anyone about anything, fearful of his or her disapproval? Now, if you're a pastor and you answered yes, then you are in trouble, because you will spend your entire ministry in bondage to what I will term in this chapter as *they*.

Looking back over my thirty-plus years of ministry, I can remember so many times, especially in those early years, when a disgruntled member would come to me with a grievance and then say, "And I'm not the only one. *They* feel the same way." As a young pastor, *they*—whoever they were—gave me the jitters. They sounded like an unruly bunch, the kind of folks who could be easily provoked. In fact, such a member would often confide that he wanted to save me from much heartache and help me learn how to make "they" happy.

But—and there is a big *but* here—I just couldn't put my finger on "they." I called the FBI (just joking), enlisted leaders, asked church members, and rounded up a posse trying to find "they." I wanted to reason with this group or at least to know who they were. However, in time I discovered that these members who came as a representative of "they" were actually the lone ranger. In other words, the annoyed member wanted to frighten me by letting me know that there were others who felt the same way. There weren't.

This practice—which, I might add, was effective for a while—

reminded me of a man who went to look at a frog farm. The owner took him out late in the evening to listen to what seemed to be a symphony of healthy, ready-to-eat frogs. The buyer made the purchase and drained the pond, only to discover one lone bullfrog making all the racket. Too often, the church and her leaders are muscled into silence by her critics—and imaginary ones at that.

Dave Ramsey says about criticism, "You can count on criticism if you do anything of scale that matters. You can't be afraid of criticism. It comes with the territory. Yet I've met people who won't stand for justice and make a decision because someone somewhere might be upset. Instead you should just count on someone not liking the call you make." Ramsey goes on to say this about his own organization: "We will consider with wisdom who might not like something and work to build consensus on decisions, but at the end of the day, fear of gripes from do-nothing people or the opposition isn't going to keep the Entre-Leader from making the call" (Ramsey, 2011, 60).

Ramsey understands that effective leaders are those who do not base their decisions on the shouts of the disenchanted. Pastors and church leaders who decide to confront must not cower down under the threat of criticism, because there is no end to the critics that are sure to surface throughout the process of confrontation. Ramsey concludes, "Aristotle said, 'There is only one way to avoid criticism: do nothing, say nothing, and be nothing.' The more you do, the more someone will have something negative to say … As much media as I do and as large as our brand has become, we can bale our hate mail. It goes with the territory; don't let that keep you from making the call" (Ramsey, 2011, 60).

So, why are we reluctant to confront people? Why do we shy away from speaking openly and honestly to those who may be living lifestyles that are damaging to both themselves and others? And more importantly, why are churches, which by their nature are called to be confrontational, hesitant to address members who live in habitual disobedience? The answer is: fear of criticism. In fact, in my research I was surprised to discover leaders and laity alike who feared not only the reaction of their church but even of their community. I could understand fearing the repercussions among church members, but I couldn't understand the fear of the larger community, the nonbelievers. Pastors were confessing to me that much of their apprehension was not so much over their own congregations but the community. One minister responded, "They will not like this, and worse, they will see us as judgmental." Keep in mind that "judgmental" is a favorite term used by the world to beat up the church and pressure the followers of Christ into overlooking blatant public sin.

Now, before you judge this frightened pastor, think about your own actions. Don't you often ignore ungodly behavior by professing Christians, for example, in your workplace because of fear? In other words, aren't you afraid they won't like you? Now, multiply "you" by thousands, and you have entire congregations today who choose to maneuver clear of any form of confrontation because it may result in disapproval. Churches and leaders—and yes, you and I—are convinced that our reputations will be harmed. Again, as one pastor said, "They won't like us." I asked him, "Who are *they*?" His response was, "You know, *they*, those people out there in the community."

Wow. Churches and their leaders disregard biblical standards and forfeit purity on the altar of popularity. Pastors steer clear of confrontation, convinced that it would give their church a "black eye." They are afraid that future efforts to evangelize the community—or their own images, for that matter—will be damaged, gagging them into silence. We want to be seen as kind and tolerant of those who may be living in open rebellion to the commands of Scripture. We don't want to give up our popularity for the sake of a biblical principle.

In an interesting book entitled *ReJesus: A Wild Messiah for a Missional Church*, Michael Hurst and Alan Hirsch speak to this insipid desire to be liked. "For many suburban, middle-class churches, niceness is the supreme expression of discipleship. But any cursory reading of the Gospels will serve to remind you that Jesus wasn't always all that nice. He was good. He was loving. He was compassionate. But He wasn't always nice. The church must abandon its preference for good manners and piety, and adopt again the kingdom values as taught by Jesus" (Frost and Hirsch, 2009, 184).

Many church leaders and Christians see this as an effort to be merciful, to tolerate a measure of disobedience in the hope that over time a person will repent. This attitude is much like a first-century church located in a place called Thyatira. Jesus admonished their leniency. "I know your works, your love and faith and service and patient endurance, and that your latter works exceed the first. But I have this against you, that you tolerate that woman Jezebel, who calls herself a prophetess and is teaching and seducing my servants to practice immorality and to eat food sacrificed to idols. I gave her time to repent, but she refuses to repent of her sexual immorality" (Revelation 2:19–22 ESV).

Jesus used the words "that you tolerate." Here was a congregation that had grown accustomed to the behavior of one of her members: a woman who, though she sung in the choir and served on the missions committee, was living in direct violation to the teachings of Scripture. Yes, she was still enjoying the full fellowship of the church, and for Jesus, that was a problem. Think about it. This church was yielding to immorality, accepting a lifestyle that ran contrary to Scripture. Perhaps, from what we are able to conclude from Scripture, Jezebel had a following both in the church and outside it. Church leaders may have been unwilling to address her lifestyle because of the damage it would inflict on their own reputations within the community. They, like so many churches today, wanted to shy away from the conflict that would be generated by confronting her. Who wants negative publicity?

Are you shocked by their reaction? Let me bring it closer to home. You work in the office with someone who, though claiming to be a Christian, is living a soap opera. And rather than confronting them, you prefer the notoriety of being gracious and willing to overlook such a lifestyle. Note again Jesus' words to this church: "that you tolerate." To tolerate someone or something is to put up with the person or their actions when you know deep down inside that they are wrong. Though they may be annoying us, we continue to endure the annoyance. Who wants criticism?

Killing the Church

Today the church is tolerating a lot for "they." In fact, many are sacrificing scripturally sound, morally responsible behavior on the altar of tolerance—a direction fueled, no doubt, by the desire of churches to be liked and accepted by both their congregations and their communities. Christians gather under the banner of tolerance, reevaluating longstanding biblical positions in an effort to gain public approval. Churches claim to have new revelations on moral issues as culture mounts pressure. They forget that once they compromise on these issues there is little desire to jeopardize their newfound popularity. "They," the general population, then drives the leadership and the church. Remember: if we promote the approval of "they" over the scriptural integrity of our doctrine or preaching, then there will be a great cost to us all.

I believe it was Tom Landry, the former coach of the Dallas Cowboys, who said, "Never let your critics plan your agenda," the thought being that once you go down the slippery path of seeking approval from those who you wish to influence, you will in time forfeit your ability to lead. The decisions of a pastor—or, for that matter, any believer—are not to be governed or guided by the approval of community but rather by the counsel of Scriptures. Once you are more concerned about what others think than by what the Scriptures mandate, then you are a prisoner to—you guessed it—"they."

Let me bring this a little closer to home. If you are more concerned about being liked than you are about being loyal to your faith, then you will tolerate much in the way of disobedience. You will excuse people's lifestyles, though they may be blatantly immoral. The person with whom you work who claims to be Christian will live a depraved life while you remain silent. Why? Because you want to be liked, or because you've convinced yourself that to confront them will only damage that person or those you wish to evangelize. No, the truth is that we don't like sitting alone in the break room, nor do we like the name tag "judgmental." I hear what you mean: "They won't like me."

In his devotional book, *Uncommon Life Daily Challenge*, Tony Dungy, the former coach of the Indianapolis Colts, comments, "*Twelve Angry*

Men is one of my favorite movies. Henry Fonda plays a juror in a murder trial, and the evidence seems so clear-cut that the other eleven jurors are ready to return a guilty verdict. But Fonda's character isn't satisfied with the evidence and wants to go through it again—and again and again. Every time a vote is taken, he stands alone. The other jurors are impatient and ready to move on, and some turn the disagreement into a personal battle. But he keeps his focus on the job, urges them to reexamine the case, and points out the gaps in the evidence. The votes begin to shift. Eventually, all the jurors agree on a not-guilty verdict." Dungy continues, "It's hard to stand alone against popular opinion" (Dungy, 2011, August 15). And I love Dungy's quote by Chuck Noll: "Stubbornness is a virtue—if you're right!" (Dungy, 2011, August 15). Let's admit it. It is hard to stand against popular opinion. Coaches like Dungy understand well the pressure of critics and the danger of giving in to that pressure. Likewise, every pastor must know the constant tension of his position and refuse the control of his critics.

Lee Iacocca says about leaders, "You have to face the problems head-on while they're happening, or they build up and become catastrophes" (Iacocca and Whitney, 2007, 192). The danger is when church leaders and laity overlook insubordination because they long for acceptance, to be liked by "they." Jesus was making it clear to the church and her leaders at Thyatira that it was not their right to "tolerate" the behavior of this disobedient member. If someone was slapping you in the face and I said, "I am tolerating this abuse," your response would be, "It's not your face that's being slapped." Jesus never told us to tolerate public, willful, habitual patterns of sin but rather to confront them and lead them to repentance.

Now, with that in mind, let's admit that the world loves a tolerant church, one in which the membership's lifestyles are ignored. But why? Why does the world bully the church into mediocrity and threaten her with its disapproval? And when did the church start caring? Undoubtedly, Paul wasn't too upset over Rome's disapproval. When did we start wanting the accolades of the world, and why does the world push for the church to be more tolerant? If nonbelievers don't accept our belief system, why are they so concerned and critical about how we address disobedience? Could it be because a nonconfrontational church or Christian is of little or no threat to the lifestyles of the community? When a church muscles up against "they" and addresses, for example, immorality within her membership, she is confronting not only the behavior of her congregants but the behavior of the entire community. Read that last sentence again.

Let me illustrate. Suppose you are eating out with another family. Your children are seated with your neighbor's children at an adjacent table, while you and your friends are engrossed in conversation. The children, unbeknownst to the adults, are beginning to get loud and messy. Several customers appear annoyed and look in your direction to see if you or your friends are going to deal with the situation. After several glares, mumbling, and clearing of throats, you notice the insubordination and correct it. Now the question becomes, will your friends do the same with their children? Thankfully, they follow suit. But let me ask you: why? What happened? Why did your neighbors, who might have a more liberal view of parenting, feel pressured to discipline their own children? Did your demand for a higher standard of behavior in your children's conduct compel them to do likewise? Did your disciplining of your children's behavior say to them, *Your children's behavior is also inappropriate?*

When the church confronts unethical or immoral behavior in their members, it is in essence saying something to the community: "If you (community) behave the way this member is behaving, then your behavior is wrong." Consequently, the world dislikes a church that takes confrontation and discipline seriously and loves a church that does not.

I saw an editorial reprint that was interesting. "The role of the church as the prophetic critic of society is neglected today; instead, the chief emphasis is on the healing ministry of the church, on Christianity as the antidote for anxiety, on the gospel's promise of peace of mind. There is a prophetic "no" which still needs to be said, but there is a tendency to omit it, in part because of the preoccupation with the "positive" message and in part because in the nation's present state of mind prophetic criticism is more that unusually misunderstood or resented. Again, when any congregation confronts members who are living contrary to Scripture, they are in fact confronting everyone. If you speak to the professing believer who works in your office about his or her conduct, you are in essence speaking to everyone. So, no wonder the unchurched scream for "tolerance" (Fey and Frakes, 1962, 47–48). Let me add that the reason this editorial was interesting was because of its date: January 6, 1954. Reluctance to confront disobedience has, and will always be, resented by those outside the church.

The emerging New Testament church was adamant about confronting disobedience. The early church fathers confronted unbiblical behavior, regardless of the reaction of the communities in which they were found. They knew what modern day leaders have forgotten—that if the community planned the church's agenda, they were in trouble. In other words, if members or leaders could live outside the dictates of Scripture without any disciplinary action being taken, then the cause of Christ would be sabotaged and the Great Commission undermined. This is why we find the larger portion of the apostolic writings confrontational in style.

For example, Corinth was a wicked city, and yet Paul openly and aggressively dealt with moral issues within the membership. He relentlessly prodded even her emerging leaders to maintain purity and holiness at every juncture. Keep in mind that the community of Corinth was the Las Vegas of her day and full of the grossest depravity. And yet Paul could not allow the approval of "they" to override scriptural authority. Had Paul's letter to the church at Corinth been published in the local paper, there would have been an outcry against this narrow-minded, bigoted believer. There would have been a community-wide effort to squelch his and the church's influence. Why? Because when Paul addressed the member's moral conduct, he was addressing all of Corinth.

The standard must be upheld, regardless of the community's reaction. The community cannot be the authority to which the children of God go for approval or accountability. If the church wants the approval of the community, then the community will become the ones to whom the church is accountable. If I want your approval, then in some ways I become accountable to you. "Am I pleasing you?" becomes the driving force of my life. For example, if I work for you, then it would be safe to say that I will want to please you. If I want to please you, then I will come to you to see if I am doing so. Therefore, I am accountable to you. The church that seeks community approval will constantly go to the community to see how it is doing. In essence, we report to the ones we wish to please.

In their book, *The Leadership Secrets of Billy Graham*, Harold Myra and Marshall Shelley spoke of a meeting in Modesto, California, that would change and protect the ministry of Billy Graham throughout its tenure. "So one afternoon during the Modesto meetings, Billy called the team together to discuss the problem. 'God has brought us to this point,' he said. 'Maybe he is preparing us for something that we don't know. Let's try to recall all the things that have been a stumbling block and a hindrance to evangelists in years past, and let's come back together in an hour and talk about it and pray about it and ask God to guard us from them.' The meeting would culminate in an agreement that each man could, if need be, confront the other" (Myra and Shelley, 2005, 54).

Billy Graham recognized that the ability to confront and hold each other to the highest level of ethical standards was critical to their ministry. This discipline could not be put in the hands of the listener, the crowds, or the larger community but rather in the hands of each team member. If we are called upon to be an element of change, we cannot expect or seek the approval of those we wish to change. If we do, then we will find ourselves accountable to them as well. For example, if an elementary school teacher is more concerned over her approval rating by her students then she is over their learning, both she and the class are in trouble. Again, the standard must be upheld, regardless of the community's reaction.

A good example of this is Paul's encounter with Peter. Let me quickly tell the story, which is found in Galatians 2:11–21. A delegation of church leaders from Jerusalem had been sent to investigate Gentile converts. Keep in mind that the Jews still wrestled with these pagans coming to Christ. Peter, who had until this time been all chummy with the Gentile believers, was now pulling back, more concerned about the approval of the Jewish elites than he was with these new believers. You would have thought Paul would play it safe and go along with Peter, knowing that the approval of these Jerusalem leaders was critical. Not hardly. Paul would not neglect confronting a brother who was wrong, even if it meant that "they," who were the apostolic fathers, didn't like it. He confronted Peter to his face, publicly admonishing him for his hypocrisy in relation to his treatment of new Gentile Christians.

Paul wrote, "When Peter came to Antioch, I opposed him to his face, because he was clearly in the wrong. Before certain men came from James, he used to eat with the Gentiles. But when they arrived, he began to draw back and separate himself from the Gentiles because he was afraid of those who belonged to the circumcision group. The other Jews joined him in his hypocrisy, so that by their hypocrisy even Barnabas was led astray. *When I saw* that they were not acting in line with the truth of the gospel, *I said* to Peter *in front of them all*, 'You are a Jew, yet you live like a Gentile and not like a Jew. How is it, then, that you force Gentiles to follow Jewish customs?" (Galatians 2:11–14 NIV).

Note how Paul said, "I opposed him to his face." This is an immediate and public confrontation, with no fear of "they." Paul said that "he [Peter] was clearly in the wrong." The word *clearly* implies a public act of disobedience on Peter's part that required a public confrontation by Paul. Note also that this act was influencing others; "the other Jews joined him." Had Paul chosen to remain silent, hesitant to intervene for fear of others, there could have been severe damage to the early church. Again, in the emerging New Testament church, confrontation was normal and could not be neglected for fear of disapproval from the community or even the church. "They" was not a factor in considering when and if the church confronted disobedience. Allow me one more example.

Was Jesus any different? Was he reluctant to confront or worried about the community's disapproval or the criticism that would come? No. In fact, Jesus would take confrontation to a whole new level, probing into the very thoughts of his critics and his followers. Imagine that! Even a man's private thoughts were not above his scrutiny. For example, and you'll love this, Simon, a Pharisee, had invited Jesus to his home for a meal. Listen to this confrontation.

> Now one of the Pharisees invited Jesus to have dinner with him, so he went to the Pharisee's house and reclined at the table. When a woman who had lived a sinful life in that town learned that Jesus was eating at the Pharisee's house, she brought an alabaster jar of perfume, and as she stood behind him at his feet, weeping, she began to wet his feet with her tears. Then she wiped them with her hair, kissed them, and poured perfume on them. When the Pharisee who had invited him saw this, he said to himself, 'If this man were a prophet, he would know who is touching him and what kind of woman she is, that she is a sinner.'
>
> Jesus answered him, "Simon, I have something to tell you."
>
> "Tell me, teacher," he said.
>
> "Two men owed money to a certain moneylender. One owed him five hundred denarii, and the other fifty. Neither of them had the money to pay him back, so he canceled the debts of both. Now, which of them will love him more?"
>
> Simon replied, "I suppose the one who had the bigger debt canceled."
>
> "You have judged correctly," Jesus said. (Luke 7:36–43 NIV, emphasis mine)

Notice the wording, "he said to himself." Clearly Simon was reflecting on the scene transpiring in front of him, coming to the conclusion that if Jesus knew the heart of man, he would know what kind of woman this was who knelt at his feet. Simon was clearly guilty of passing judgment on a woman he did not even know. Jesus' question to Simon not only demonstrated his knowledge of the woman but of the mental reflections of the man to whom he was a guest. Here we find confrontation at a whole new level, along with the principle that *sin should be confronted, regardless.* Jesus never allowed sin to go unnoticed. He confronted sin in any shape, form, or fashion, which is a far cry from today's church. And Jesus was not concerned about the approval of others who were in attendance at Simon's home. He would not allow the criticism of his opponents to dictate his response.

There are other examples of Jesus confronting the thoughts of individuals, even among his followers. His disciples could be deep in controversy over, for example, which of them was the greatest, only to have him interrupt with, "What were you arguing about?"

"An argument started among the disciples as to which of them would be the greatest. *Jesus, knowing their thoughts*, took a little child and had him stand beside him. Then he said to them, 'Whoever welcomes this little child in my name welcomes me; and whoever welcomes me welcomes the one who sent me. For he who is least among you all—he is the greatest'" (Luke 9:46–50 NIV, emphasis mine). Jesus would not allow sin to go unchallenged. Notice that even their thoughts were not above confrontation. He did something that annoys my wife when I say, "I know what you're thinking." The tragedy of today's church is that we ignore blatant disobedience because we don't want the battle or because we fear the reprisal of those in the company of the offender. Do you?

Helping the Laity: Confronting When Worried about What Others Think

For most of us, there is this desire to be liked, to have approval, but once we take seriously the responsibility of watching over the relationships that surround us, then trouble will surely come. The truth is that we often overlook destructive behavior because we don't want someone to think badly of us. We want his approval more than we want the well-being of that friend. I know that hurts, but in many cases, it is true. We may know that what a friend is doing will in time result in heartache, yet we refuse to address it because of the isolation that is sure to come.

You know what I mean. You speak to a friend about a lifestyle choice that is contrary to Scripture, only to be labeled the villain. Your friend, who is now hurt by your confronting him, corrals all your mutual acquaintances to share *just* how much you have hurt him. Remember the young person in the first chapter who, after much prayer and counsel, stepped up to confront an inappropriate relationship between her youth pastor and a female leader? She ended up being ostracized and alienated by leaders and youth alike. What's interesting is that our friends will often agree with us privately but are unwilling to take a stand publicly. And to make matters worse, they will often betray us because they are so desperate for acceptance themselves.

There is a principle here: those who confront must always be ready to stand alone. In the Old Testament, prophets were called to be confronters. The task was lonely and often brought isolation and separation from the communities in which they lived. Likewise, churches that take their responsibilities seriously may find themselves alienated from their communities, sister churches, and even denominations. Let's admit it. There is a desire in all of us to be liked, to want people to think well of us. Who would intentionally try to make enemies?

Yet if you and I confront sin, we will have no shortage of enemies. I used to struggle with this in the early years of ministry, and I still do. As I mentioned earlier, confrontation has cost my family and me. Thinking back, there were times when some people made it clear that my death would be the best news they could receive. Wow! The thought of people celebrating at my funeral bothered me. While my family was mourning, other people would be throwing a party.

I remember when Jerry Falwell's death was announced. Talk about a man who understood community disapproval! When he died, a variety of groups almost immediately hit the streets, marching in parades, celebrating his death. In his book, *The Next Christians*, Gabe Lyons quoted Christopher Hitchens, a renowned atheist, in his summation of Jerry Falwell's life in a CNN interview.

> Cooper: I'm not sure you believe in heaven, but if you do, do you think Jerry Falwell is in it?
>
> Hitchens: No, and I think it's a pity that there isn't a hell for him to go to.
>
> Cooper: What is it about him that brings up such vitriol?
>
> Hitchens: The empty life of this ugly little charlatan proves only one thing: that you can get away with the most extraordinary offenses to morality and to truth in this country if you will just get yourself called reverend.
>
> Cooper: Whether you agree or not with his reading of the Bible, you don't think he was sincere in what he spoke?
>
> Hitchens: No. I think if he read the Bible at all—and I doubt that he could actually read any long book at all—that he did so only in the most hucksterish, as we say, Bible-pounding way. (Lyons, 2010, 15)

I thought as I read this interview, *Is this the cost of confrontation?* Would any prophet of the Old Testament or historical figure from the New Testament have received any different treatment had they lived in our day? Maybe it's easier when "they" simply don't approve. The bottom line is this: if a minister lives for the approval of "they," he will live in bondage, and he will never achieve all that God would have done with his life and the lives of those he was called to minister to. He will constantly avoid criticism for fear of the disproval of his critics, which is sure to come. In his attempt to grapple for affirmation by his congregation and community, he will, in the end, make himself accountable to the very audience he has been called to change.

CHAPTER 8

Confrontation: What Kind of Behavior Requires It?

I ATTENDED A FUNERAL A WHILE back where a friend had been hired to officiate. While standing in line, waiting to view the body, he came up and spoke to my wife and me. His breath was so strong that I thought if he got close to the casket we could have a resurrection. We didn't know if we were in a funeral home or an Italian restaurant. We chalked it up to a supper that no amount of gum, toothpaste, or mouthwash could cover. However, the next day at the funeral service, we found the same breath. Surely he had not eaten the leftovers for breakfast. The smell of garlic was so strong that it was almost amusing to watch the guests as they encountered the wrath of Italy. Afterward, my wife and I concluded that his breath, probably scented by a garlic pill that would help his heart, was about to stop ours. Now the question was, would we address it? Don't we all have bad breath at times? And what if he looked at me and said, "Your breath is not necessarily a pleasant experience either"?

Let's face it: we are all sinners. All of us are guilty, and we all have bad breath occasionally. No one is innocent, so how can anyone, including a church, know who should or should not be confronted? What type of behavior warrants the involvement of others—or for that matter, an entire church? If confrontation is taught and developed among its members, then how is leadership to determine who should be confronted?

There is great danger in members running out of the sanctuary after a pastor's sermon on confrontation and inflicting worse damage. Such congregants see themselves as self-appointed deputies, flashing their badges and policing the masses. Why do some offenders go unnoticed, quietly allowed to live in rebellion, while others are confronted and corrected? Whom do you confront?

I think we must constantly be warned to believe the best about a person. Nelson Mandela said, "People will feel that I see too much good in people. So it's a criticism I have to put up with and I've tried to adjust to, because whether it is so or not, it is something, which I think is profitable. It's a good thing to assume, to act on the basis that … others are men of integrity and honor … because you tend to attract integrity and honor if that is how you regard those with whom you work" (Mandela, 2010, 263).

So, who *should* be confronted? Church members should be taught to examine the circumstances surrounding the unbiblical behavior in question. In other words, how and where did the offense take place? You may be wondering why that is even an issue. First, to say that we all sin is one thing, but to use that as an excuse for indifference toward disobedient lifestyles is quite another. Second, if we are to answer the question about whom to confront, then we must address the *how* and *where* of the offense.

Let me illustrate. Suppose you are in a department store browsing, when you notice two mothers engaged in separate conversations with their little boys about staying close and not wandering off. You watch as the first little boy nods in agreement, but as soon as the mom's back is turned, he sticks out his tongue. When she turns back around, he appears to be compliant, though eventually he wanders off. Now, this is critical to our discussion. You would conclude, from his behavior that though he is defiant, he did not do so in plain sight of the parent. In other words, though he stuck his tongue out, he did so with his mom's back turned. Why? His sly attempt toward insurrection was is still governed by either a level of respect or fear for the authority figure.

In the case of our second mother and son, the same parental discussion takes place. Only this time the child pulls away, sticks out his tongue, and runs off. We would deduce that this child is not only disobedient but is also much more flagrant and bold in his insurrection, demonstrating no respect or fear of his mother. Further, though both mothers failed the test (both boys wandered off), we would admire the first mom over the second. Why? Because she does hold some measure of respect and authority in the life of her child. Moreover, we would also conclude that the first mother's chances of seeing her son to adulthood will be easier than the second mother's.

The church has always had disobedience within the ranks. Yet how the membership disobeys—as we saw with our two little boys—is crucial to our discussion. Members who wander off, slipping into the shadows in closet conspiracies, do so with some level of fear or respect for both the authority of Scripture and the church, much like our first child. However, others who flagrantly live out their rebellion in the public arena with little if any respect for the authority of Scripture or the church do so with an arrogance that causes a lost world to disrespect the authority in charge.

In essence, our fear and even danger is that our second child may represent a growing segment of today's church membership—congregants who are not only living out their rebellion but are doing so publicly. They are defiant, sticking out their tongues in the face of the authority of Scripture and the church—and worse, in front of the lost. What complicates our mission is the community of nonbelievers who, like customers in the store, are evaluating not only the rebellion of the two boys but the response of their mothers as well. In other words, once the child's rebellion has gone public, if the parent ignores the defiant behavior, then those of us who are watching will, like the child, lose respect. The world never respects any institution that is mismanaged and undisciplined. Going back to my friend with the bad breath, I thought, *Why didn't the funeral director address the issue? Why was it my place to do so?* Then I thought, *It wasn't fair that I was holding my own breath while he was unleashing his.* The answer was simple. Those in authority over him were negligent in addressing the matter.

We must ask the question: is today's church really admired by the nonbeliever for its tolerance of unbiblical behavior?

Going back to our illustration, which of the two mothers do you respect? Think about it. These mothers are really in a precarious situation, because you and I are in the store, and we have observed the exchange. What each of these mothers choose to do with their sons will determine what we think of them as mothers. (Read that sentence again.) For instance, we have already determined that the second little boy does not respect his mother. Now the question is, will we? Keep in mind that if the church fails to discipline a member, instead extending the full privileges of membership, then the church is actually rewarding the behavior. This would be like the second mom rewarding her son's insubordination with an ice cream cone while we look on! What would you think?

So, what kind of sin warrants intervention? The answer is, if you have not already guessed it: the kind of sin that has become habitual and is lived out in the public arena with no respect for the authority in charge.

Perhaps this was how Paul felt as he addressed the church at Corinth. In the case of gross sexual misconduct, the leadership had chosen to ignore the situation. So, as Paul wrote his first letter to the congregation, he expressed more alarm over their indifference than he did about the incest! "I can hardly believe the report about the sexual immorality going on among you, something so evil that even the pagans don't do it. I am told that you have a man in your church who is living in sin with his father's wife. *And you are proud of yourselves!* Why aren't you mourning in sorrow and shame? And *why haven't you removed this man from your fellowship?*" (1 Corinthians 5:1–2 NLT, emphasis mine). The leadership knew the immorality that was taking place, yet they refused to address it! In essence, Paul was asking, "Why aren't you upset?" Do you know any church that is mourning over the condition of its members? The behavior that warrants intervention is public behavior that is observed and known by the membership.

Why was this so critical to Paul? He saw the cancerous nature of sin and the damage done when a member had no respect for authority and lived out his insurrection in the public eye. Remember, sin never lies dormant in the believer or the church; it will spread throughout its host. Let me illustrate.

As a missionary in Zimbabwe, Africa, I was traveling with a companion who stopped at a local bush hospital to make a visit. A black mamba, an African snake, had bitten a small boy in a neighboring village. This particular snake is considered to be one of the most notorious on the continent. When threatened, it will lift the greater portion of its body and strike with a venom that can kill in minutes. The doctor escorted us to the ward where, on a bed near the nurse's station, lay the frail figure of a boy no more than eight years of age. Though the boy was alive, his right arm was swollen, the flesh rotting in such a way that it was almost nauseating. When my friend questioned the condition of the boy, the doctor responded, "His arm is threatening his body." I thought to myself, *What a theological truth!*

In much the same way, American churches are encumbered by a growing membership that, though they may claim salvation, are in reality diseased appendages hanging limp, deformed, and rotting. A spiritual rather than pathological condition threatens the general health of the organism. If sin is lived out in the public arena to the degree that it becomes a *lifestyle of disobedience*, it will, given time, threaten the health of the larger body of believers and so must be addressed.

The kind of behavior that is to be confronted is the kind that is public and lived out in a defiant, in-your-face manner. Because the world watches, the church is in a catch-22, a paradox of sorts. On the one hand, the world refuses to respect an institution that fails to control the behavior of their members, while on the other hand, they react when we do confront and discipline the members in question. Leaders must understand that when the church exercises confrontation and perhaps discipline, she will be ridiculed either way. Much like a parent who is forced to discipline his child in public, we must accept that this as the cost of confrontation and correction. In fact, most parents understand that a child, given the chance, will play this card in public. Children know that their parents would prefer not to draw attention or, as some would say, "make a scene."

Church members are no different. They too bank on the fact that the church would prefer to avoid a scene (except, maybe, in the case of clergy). For example, consider our illustration of two mothers correcting their child in a store. Those observers who, moments earlier, might have been thinking, *Why can't she control her child?* are now thinking, *She is abusive and cruel.* Once one of these mothers confronts and corrects her child in public, she will then be judged in that same arena by a public that often sees corporal punishment or even a verbal reprimand as harsh and uncalled-for. The church must remember that this dilemma cannot frighten either parent or church into silence. True, to correct will bring a negative response, but not to do so will, over time, bring even greater consequences. The church, like the parent, must ignore the audience and act appropriately. In other words, instead of giving little Johnny what he wants to keep him quiet—and so keep the public's attention away—the parent must choose to correct, regardless of where they are or who may be watching. Likewise, the church must correct members whose unbiblical behavior has gone public.

It is safe to say that critical to the health and even survival of a church is her refusal to succumb to the world's pressure. She must not conform to a level of acceptance that, though appeasing at the moment, wreaks havoc in the end. In other words, the world may not understand what is at stake, but the church does.

Let me also add that if the rebellious child in the illustration is not my own, I may be content to merely watch the show, thankful that the little tyke is of no relation. However, if I knew that this child would one day grow up and, years down the road, break into my home and harm my family, I might think differently about this mother's disciplinary process.

The implication is much the same with an audience of nonbelievers who are witnessing a local church confronting inappropriate behavior. The average citizen does not comprehend the cost when the church fails to hold its members to biblical standards. Just as the uncontrollable child could in time turn into a negative influence in the community, so too can a church member. The world has no comprehension of how critical confrontation and discipline may be to their own well-being! Remember that the church acts like salt as a preservative agent in society. If the salt loses it preservative quality, then we are all in trouble.

What About the Label of Hypocrite?

Church members who are being confronted will often come back at the church with the often-used word *hypocrite*. The term is wielded like a weapon to ward off the confrontational voice, to silence the authorities or to put them on the defensive. Let's face it: the label frightens many would-be confronters, because they know that it is true. People do feel like hypocrites. *Who am I to speak to someone about his life when I have such a difficult time with my own?* So the general public, as well as wayward members, attack the disciplinary hand as either unsympathetic or, worse, hypocritical. The truth is, we know that the best of members wrestle with some form of sin and could be labeled a hypocrites. But in the case of those who are to be confronted, the behavior of the member has gelled into a *pattern* of *willful, flagrant, public* sin that, if allowed to continue, will undermine the mission of the church.

Though the cost may be great, public and willful defiance that evolves into a lifestyle must be confronted if the church is to have any hope of reaching a lost world. Pastors must know that this kind of sin, more than any other, affects the strength of the church. It dilutes her effectiveness and will, given time, weaken her testimony.

What Is Our Standard?

We could not conclude this subject without mentioning that our standard of conduct in the life of the church is the Word of God. Its moral and ethical principles provide the guidelines by which we are able to judge whether a certain behavior is deemed inappropriate. Today, churches pressured by the culture are vacillating, appearing to doubt whether a particular sin in question is clearly addressed in Scripture. In other words, society has exerted such influence that the local church buckles under the pressure and conforms to what for centuries has been a given and enters into a "new enlightenment." Every local congregation must fight the urge to give in, to disregard the original intent of Scripture. In most moral issues of our day, church leadership for centuries has understood the Scripture and taught accordingly. To ignore it or to reposition the church is to make the God of Scripture appear to be unsure himself, vacillating between opinions. This brings up another question in our modern day.

Is Obedience a Choice?

If obedience is seen as a choice, then the church will never confront. In his interesting book, *Hot Tub Religion*, J. I. Packer said, "We are much more interested in something called 'emotional maturity,' which encourages moral tolerance with no emphasis on behavioral standards. In our passion for intimacy with God and our boldness in treating Him as a pal, we are reacting against the stress on His holiness and His demand that those who seek His face be holy, too" (Packer, 1987, 168). Note the words "with no emphasis on behavioral standards."

Once the church compromises on obedience, confrontation is a relic of the past. Moral tolerance becomes the banner cry, and those who would attempt to question congregational behavior are labeled *pharisaic*. In fear, leadership cowers down, intimidated by the masses. We forget, as Packer goes on to say, "though we are not under the law as a system of salvation, we are divinely directed to keep it … There is no happiness without holiness" (Packer, 1987, 168).

Frances A. Schaffer said, "Christians must not let the world defile them. If the world sees us conforming to its standards and relativism, it will not listen to whatever we say. It will have no reason to" (Schaffer, 1974, 25). Why? Because we are just like them.

Obedience is not a choice. In fact, "God clarifies in the midst of obedience, not beforehand" (McManus, 2002, 57). Perhaps the growing awareness of the need among laity to discover purpose and meaning is and has always been wrapped up in childlike obedience. Again, obedience is not an option but a command, and the lack of it affects the whole body. Erwin McManus goes on to say, "Faith is trusting God enough to obey what He has said, and hope is having the confidence that God will do everything he has promised … It's better to tame a wild stallion than it is to ride a dead horse" (McManus, 2002, 150).

George Buttrick once said, "As we have in our large cities a 'Bureau of Missing Persons,' it might be well if we had also a 'Bureau of Missing Words.' Has anyone missed a word of late? It is rarely mentioned. A conspiracy of silence seems to have closed in on it like a muffling, blinding fog. It is the word 'obedience'" (Rees, 1969, 53).

For the Laity: When Should You Confront?

Confrontation should be done only where there is clear violation to a Scriptural directive. When a friend's behavior has evolved into a lifestyle that is contrary to Scripture and you have personal, firsthand knowledge about it, you are then to proceed with confrontation. You must understand that once you enter into the lives of others, there will come a feeling of isolation from mutual friends. By that, I mean that the friend being confronted will reach out for support, surrounding himself or herself with supporters who will see you, the confronter, as mean-spirited and unfair. There is no way around it. Regardless of your attempts to be kind and understanding, you will pay a cost for the encounter.

Keep in mind that whoever is confronting should not be guilty of the same offenses. If you are, then don't be surprised when the one being confronted—along with others—quickly and accurately label you a hypocrite. However, if you have come to a level of victory in a particular area that is now threatening a friend, then use that as a source of encouragement and a reason for concern. Your standard should be, as it is for the church, the Word of God.

CHAPTER 9

Confrontation Must Be Seasoned With Grace

CONDOLEEZZA RICE SHARES ABOUT HER first time meeting President George H. W. Bush. "My first face-to-face encounter with the president was wonderful. He was kind and thanked me profusely for everything that I'd done. 'You're so good to agree to leave California and help me out,' he said. *Is he kidding?* I thought. *He's the president.* But I learned that day, and would see throughout my time with him, that this wasn't false modesty: George H. W. Bush is simply one of the nicest and most self-effacing people that I've ever met. He taught me so much about leading people" (Rice, 2010, 248). Church leadership must demonstrate the same kindness as they model discipline of the church. Confrontation without kindness is detrimental to the overall health of any church. To confront people with kindness is the surest hope for real reconciliation.

As a boy growing up, I remember those times when I was instructed by a parent to go and cut a switch for the discipline of one of my siblings. Looking back, I realize that I relished the personal satisfaction of scoping out the backyard for the largest instrument possible, thankful that I would not be on the receiving end of it. For some in the church there is the same tendency, a delight at the opportunity to address the behavior of a fellow church member. Perhaps a good rule of thumb would be this: if someone delights in "cutting a switch," they are disqualified from the process of confrontation.

With this in mind, every pastor must continually caution the church to season confrontation with grace. Why? Because a congregation will leave a sermon on confrontation with their Bible and bat. People will—if the leadership is not careful—barrel out the doors of the church to enjoy the personal gratification that confrontation brings to their uneventful lives, relishing the momentary interruption of conviction in their own hearts. It reminds me of elementary school when the teacher who was eyeing my conduct was distracted by another student committing a worse offense. In other words, the long arm of the law was now reaching in another direction, and I was rejoicing because it had turned away from my desk.

Beyond this, there may be a little Pharisee in all of us. In other words, we like the task of invading other people's lives, pointing out their failures, and calling them on the carpet. It makes us feel better about ourselves. We hear a voice deep down inside our soul, whispering, "You're not so bad after all." While one hand is in the face of the offender, the other is patting us on the back and giving us a "that-a-boy." Our personal worth is now drawn from the failure of another, so we not only confront, but we do so with great zeal. Again the question is this: with all of this flesh getting in the way, is it even possible for confrontation to be merciful? Or is this just an ugly task ignored by the church?

The longer I study the subject, the more convinced I am that it does not have to be cruel; it can and must be done with grace. Paul warned those at Galatia to be careful and understand that only those at the deepest level of spiritual maturity should be entrusted with this task. He counseled the Galatians, "Brothers, if someone is caught in a sin, you who are spiritual should restore him gently. But watch yourself, or you also may be tempted" (Galatians 6:1 NIV). Why would Paul stress this character trait? Because he understood the tendency toward harshness when one is put in the position of confronting a believer living in disobedience.

An excellent example of confronting is that of the Old Testament prophet Nathan. The story goes like this. King David, perhaps one of the most pivotal figures in Israel's history, had relinquished the command of his troops to others and had remained in Jerusalem to hang around the palace. On one particular evening as he reclined on his rooftop, he noticed a young woman named Bathsheba bathing. Captivated by her beauty, he called for his servants to invite her to the palace. This one-night lapse in judgment resulted in a pregnancy. Now, rather than admit his impropriety and come clean, he instead began a massive cover-up.

The king brought Bathsheba's husband, Uriah, home from the battlefield in the hope that he would sleep with his own wife. But Uriah had far greater integrity than the king. He refused to enjoy that privilege while his fellow soldiers were in the midst of a war. David did everything in his power to get Uriah in bed with Bathsheba but to no avail. Finally in desperation, he sent a message to Uriah's commander, "Put Uriah on the front line in the most intense part of the fighting and pull back the troops and leave him there alone." Soon word returned that Uriah was dead and the king was off the hook. Then King David stepped in, married the distraught widow, and moved her into the palace. Everything appeared to have gone over without a hitch—until Nathan the prophet showed up to tell David of a horrible injustice.

The prophet confronted the king by unfolding a made-up story of cruelty. He told of a local, wealthy rancher who, while entertaining guests, sent his servants to confiscate his neighbor's pet lamb. The outcome is that the poor family's little lamb is slaughtered and served on the rich man's table. And to make matters worse, the poor family has little if any recourse.

With the background set, Nathan confronts the king of Israel. Note how he incorporates a measure of savvy without being cruel.

> The Lord sent Nathan to David. When he came to him, he said, "There were two men in a certain town, one rich and the other poor. The rich man had a very large number of

sheep and cattle, but the poor man had nothing except one little ewe lamb he had bought. He raised it, and it grew up with him and his children. It shared his food, drank from his cup, and even slept in his arms. It was like a daughter to him. Now a traveler came to the rich man, but the rich man refrained from taking one of his own sheep or cattle to prepare a meal for the traveler who had come to him. Instead, he took the ewe lamb that belonged to the poor man and prepared it for the one who had come to him."

David burned with anger against the man and said to Nathan, "As surely as the Lord lives, the man who did this deserves to die! He must pay for that lamb four times over, because he did such a thing and had no pity."

Then Nathan said to David, "You are the man." (2 Samuel 12:1–7a NIV)

Do you see and hear grace in Nathan's dealing with David? Yes, there is no doubt that he loved the king by the manner in which he handled him. It's important to note that the Scripture states, "The Lord sent Nathan to David." This implies that Nathan was under the guidance and direction of the Holy Spirit. This is critical, because there is a tendency for the one doing the correcting to be harsh, not guided by the Holy Spirit but rather by his own flesh. Barreling into the lives of others in order to "straighten them out" or "talk some sense into them" is a tragic mistake and a far cry from the grace demonstrated by our Lord. How can we guard against this? By asking some questions.

The first question must always be: *has God sent me into the life of this person?* And the second is: *did I pray over this situation prior to actually visiting this person?* I heard an old preacher say of some men in ministry, "Were they sent or did they just went?" In other words, did God send them, or did they just take it upon themselves to go? Instead of being spiritually appointed, they were self-appointed. This is the never-ending temptation of those who seek to confront others. They forge ahead in the flesh and come across as irritated and angry. This presents the one doing the confronting as Pharisaic rather than Christlike, as he is not under the guidance of the Holy Spirit. Pastors must continually stress this as they guide their congregation toward greater involvement in the lives of those who may in fact need confronting.

A good New Testament example of confrontation with grace is Jesus' handling of the adulterous woman. Note how he addresses the magnitude of her sin while demonstrating grace.

> The teachers of the law and the Pharisees brought in a woman caught in adultery. They made her stand before the group and said to Jesus, "Teacher, this woman was caught in the act of adultery. In the Law, Moses commanded us to stone such women. Now what do you say?" They were using this question as a trap, in order to have a basis for accusing him.
>
> But Jesus bent down and started to write on the ground with his finger. When they kept on questioning him, he straightened up and said to them, "If any one of you is without sin, let him throw a stone at her." Again he stooped down and wrote on the ground. At this, those who heard began to go away one at a time, the older ones first, until only Jesus was left, with the woman still standing there.
>
> Jesus straightened up and asked her, "Woman, where are they? Has no one condemned you?" "No one, sir," she said. "Then neither do I condemn you," Jesus declared. "Go now and leave your life of sin." (John 8:3–11 NIV)

Jesus handled her with dignity. Perhaps the lesson here is that confrontation is far more effective when it is done with a tear in the eye and grace on the lips.

Recently I was in a public restaurant when a man—along with a woman I assumed was his wife—came in and sat down at an adjacent table. In the course of eating my meal and carrying on a conversation with church members who had also entered, I caught a glimpse of the gentleman's shirt. On the front of his T-shirt were photographs of women with little clothing and in suggestive poses. I must admit that initially I was angry and wanted to let him have it. After a few moments, I cooled down, yet I still felt that the man's apparel should be addressed.

As my wife and I prepared to leave, I approached his table, put my hand on his shoulder, and mentioned that I had noticed his shirt and wished to give him a pamphlet entitled, "Where Will You Spend Eternity?" I then walked away, giving him only enough time to laugh nervously.

A few days later, the church members who were still seated shared with me what had happened afterward. They said he had read the cover of the tract, leafed through the pages, and then taken his napkin and tucked it into the front of his shirt, thereby covering the nudity. The napkin remained there throughout the meal!

The point is that the confrontation did not have to be a volatile exchange. My hope was that the man I was addressing would simply admit to the inappropriateness of the shirt and seek to conceal it, which he did. *The hope of confrontation is transformation, not alienation.* Please read that last sentence again, and write it on your forehead. That statement must be constantly drilled into the heads of every church member who ventures into this discipline.

The pastor who fights for the souls of men must do so with grace, and yet this grace must never be seen as weak or vacillating. His role as shepherd is to guard over those that God has entrusted to him and to lead others to do the same. Every member must be willing to confront but must understand that the purpose is *transformation*, not *alienation*. Sheep cannot be allowed to wander from the fold on the pastor's watch, nor should any of the church membership. The tragedy is that many think conversion is the *end* of the journey, when in reality it is the *beginning*. Remember that conformity to Christ is the goal. Baptismal records mean little if the sheep are lost along the way.

Confrontation is pivotal to the role of pastor and laity alike. Like so many subjects of Scripture, confrontation is to be taught. As members seek to carry it out, it should be supervised and guided to ensure that it is never mean-spirited.

The question then becomes, *How can a pastor do this in such a way that it is redemptive?* More importantly, *how can he develop leaders who will be supportive and able to bring the procedure along with the same grace?* The answer to this may lie in church constitutions and by-laws. A congregation can avoid a variety of problems and demonstrate grace if they will incorporate into their legislative process a strong, biblically based model of confronting the membership in public sin.

To do this, the pastor might consider a study with his leadership (both staff and laity) in an attempt to bring them to a clear understanding of confrontation. He could further the educational process by developing a sermon series of the same nature for the congregation, preferably for the morning services. The pastor should not address this in an evening service or a Wednesday night study. A subject of this magnitude must be dealt with in the largest setting possible. Again, he is seeking to permeate the entire membership with a strong resolve to convert or turn back straying members and restore them to their rightful position in the body. To fail here will weaken the possibility of congregational support and will subvert grace itself.

Finally, to strengthen this process, incoming members should be trained in "new member orientation" to this biblical model and the church's commitment to it. The outcome will be new members being brought into the assembly with a clear comprehension of membership— as well as the process of confrontation and restoration if they should fall away. If incoming members know what to expect up front, they are less likely to become disenchanted—or worse, to attack the process. Again, this is not to create a church "police force" that goes out and searches homes. But it is to take seriously the issue of open and flagrant sin that threatens the reputation of the church.

Remember: churches that commit to the above will in time develop a better understanding of the dangers and even the cost of public sin. Congregations will begin to fathom the impact of godly lifestyles lived out in the community and will take seriously their contribution to the overall character of their local church. The tragedy for many members today is the failure to recognize their part in the reputation of the church. Instead they seem to be convinced that once they join, they are of little significance to the overall health of the body. This must change. (Take time to read the last three sentences again.) As we saw earlier in the case of Corinth, the membership needed to be reminded that no matter how small or insignificant a member might feel, he or she was as crucial to the overall health and functioning of the body as any other appendage.

Recently I had my gall bladder removed, and though the surgical process is now easier than it used to be, it still required much explanation before I was convinced to allow it. I know of no part of my body that I would intentionally seek to remove. My little toe may get very little respect from the rest of the body, but just let this tiny member catch the corner of the bed frame, and watch my entire body become involved. When this happens, my little, unobtrusive extremity is cradled by loving hands and scrutinized by my eyes, though in fact it could be blamed for the mishaps. All parts of my body are now involved, because they all feel the pain!

One of the reasons Paul wrote the first letter to the church at Corinth was to encourage the disciplinary process. This should remind the reader that although chapters twelve through fourteen dealt with gifts and love, they were ultimately a continuation of the call to confrontation in chapter five. Paul reminded the Corinthians that every member was important and none were to be ignored, left to themselves, or thought to be expendable. As we read a few lines back, "Congregations will fathom the impact of godly lifestyles lived out in the community and will take seriously their contribution to the overall character of their local church."

Helping the Laity: Confrontation Must Be Seasoned by Grace

Great cooks seem to understand the importance of seasoning, and so too must the church grasp that all confrontation must be seasoned with grace. Confrontation that is done without it should not be done at all.

Wow! Did you grasp that last sentence? It is *mandatory* that leadership ensure that confrontation with grace is a part of the spiritual training of every believer. Yes, laity must be trained in this spiritual discipline. No, it does not come naturally. As a layperson, you should ask your leadership to help you learn this critical component as a follower of Christ. Above all else, the purpose of confrontation is always *redemptive*, and that should be communicated constantly. Remember that the goal is to *reclaim* an individual. In his book, *Why People Fail*, Simon Reynolds gives an excellent example of the right attitude when dealing with people.

> There's a famous story about the great former manager and CEO of IBM, Thomas Watson. An employee had made a serious mistake and was summoned to Watson's office. Certain he was about to be fired, the employee sheepishly entered the business titan's office, his head held low.
>
> "I suppose this means I'm out of a job, Mr. Watson," the employee dejectedly remarked.
>
> "Are you kidding?" responded Watson. "It cost me almost a million dollars to teach you this lesson. Why would I want to get rid of you now that you've learned it?"
>
> As you can imagine, the staff member left the CEO's office uplifted and inspired." (Reynolds, 2012, 47)

CHAPTER 10

A Barrier to Confrontation: The Church Hop

HEARD OF A COMIC AND a stuttering singer who lived together in a hotel. The comic came in, and the singer said, "W-w-w-w … w-w-w-w-w …" The comic said, "Sing!," and the singer sang, "We've been robbed!"

The church has been robbed by a practice that is jokingly referred to it as the Church Hop. In fact, this seems to be the new craze among many who leap from one congregation to another. Churches vacillate up and down in attendance, acquiring new members who, for all practical purposes, evidence little thought to loyalty. These are casual acquaintances who relegate the decision of church affiliation to consideration of amenities, perks, and privileges. The outcome is a church that looks more like a crowd than a congregation. Men and women meander through church memberships with little regard, if any, to service, and they may even represent a great danger in their short tenure. They land like ducks on water into one membership, only to migrate to another.

To make matters worse, if—and this is a big *if*—a local congregation addresses the lifestyle of such a migratory member, the leadership may find the disciplinary process short-circuited when the offender simply picks up and flies to another location. The prodigal member quietly slips into another body of believers that is unaware of his discrepancy with his previous church—unless there is communication between the two churches involved. Why are members allowed to move from one congregation to another just because churches *let them*?

If this is not bad enough, competition has crept into the evangelical community. Churches now compete for members, thereby giving rebellious church-hoppers the edge. Today, most congregants know that if they are dissatisfied with their present situation, they need only move to another. They know that the next church in line will be more delighted over growth than it is with purity. So a new member may prance down the aisle like a harlot in a wedding, with a notoriously dishonest life intact. How do we change this pattern?

First, if leadership is to fix this, they cannot stutter or recoil with fear at the onslaught that is sure to come when they do. A lack of clarity is a surefire way to produce confusion inside as well as outside the church. Congregations are nervous enough about confrontation without leaders conducting the pilgrimage with deprivation and fear. If a leader appears to be vacillating and unsure, he will create a great deal of anxiety, which will result in a loss of support. This is similar to one parent who wishes to address misbehavior in his child, while the other parent appears to doubt the disciplinary action altogether. Anyone who is a parent knows how quickly a child picks up on this and begins to use it to his advantage.

Second, churches are often so glad to get new members that they are willing to disregard the standard procedure of *transfer of letter*, the process by which churches communicate and investigate the person who is seeking to join. Questions such as, *Is this person a member in good standing?* are no longer asked. Interestingly enough, parishioners have discovered what so many children of divorced parents learn—that both of these people (sister churches) who love me are, in fact, in competition."

You've seen it: a couple divorces and the kids are swapped out every other weekend. Over time, one parent—usually the one with an occasional weekend—begins to score big by providing all kinds of privileges with little semblance of discipline or responsibility. The outcome of this rivalry is that offspring wield a power that can circumvent the primary parent's authority. Parents who are in the process of raising a child can be at odds, with one parent so desiring the acceptance of the child that he disregards inappropriate behavior. Taking this illustration to the church demonstrates that the membership can manipulate the leadership. The failure of churches and denominations to understand this dynamic has weakened—and will continue to weaken—the influence of the local body of believers.

"Migrating members" are the result of a society that is increasingly transient in nature. A. Middlemann comments, "The mentality of a flight from the past, of being on the move constantly, of always seeking greener pastures elsewhere and never really settling down creates a focus on the self, the individual, and on change as a habit. The number of Christians who change their church affiliation in search of better fellowship, kinder discipline, or more entertaining programs is larger than those who remain where their parents lie buried and where they grew up" (Middlemann, 2004, 15).

This trend merely complicates confrontation, because as long as people are on the move, there is little threat of confrontation. One simply flees at the first sign of accountability. Middlemann continues, "The individual is the center of his life, with little sense of roots in land and relationships" (Middlemann, 2004, 15). So what can the church do?

Rethinking: Transfer of Membership

First, churches within the same denomination must restore the "transfer of membership" process to its original intent. Historically, the intent was to protect sister churches from parishioners who sought to move to another congregation while under church discipline or living in habitual sin that had become public knowledge. If the intent is still to protect the church, then congregations should return the induction of potential members to the business meeting rather than the end of a service and a hearty amen. Too many new members are ushered in with an *amen*, when in reality, if the new church knew what the previous church knew, it would be an *oh no*.

Second, this requires a level of integrity that many churches have compromised for the sake of expediency. Congregations will send a *transfer of letter* with no concern for a sister church. They may be so glad to get rid of a problem member that they readily send the letter. They take what was meant to be a protective device and instead dismiss it as insignificant. The outcome is that churches provide the music for the Church Hop.

I heard of a prostitute who, after sleeping with men, would get up early and slip out of the room, leaving a message in bold red lipstick: "Welcome to the family of AIDS." Law enforcement, in seeking to apprehend the assailant, considered her to be a murderer. Yet how many letters are sent by one church to another, knowing that the member in question is a dangerous infection? At best, what is happening in churches is horrible neglect; at worst, it is murder. Tragically, some churches have died cruel deaths from the induction of members that sister churches knew to be "hazardous to the health."

Third, form letters need to identify the behavior of members, such as blatant misconduct, habitual absenteeism, lack of financial commitment in the area of the tithe, or a disregard for service in general. Even in the business world, job applications contain references and correspondence with previous employers so that enough information is shared to determine whether or not the candidate is of a reputable character. Though companies may be in competition, even they maintain a level of integrity that requires a fair and honest appraisal when employees are changing jobs. Likewise, transfer-of-membership forms should do the same and may require churches to update, discuss, and vote on a better format. Leadership must involve the entire congregation in the process, helping them to understand what is required to be a "member in good standing."

Finally, all of this means nothing if churches are not willing to listen to other congregations. A church that refuses to work within the guidelines of the New Testament and instead seeks to build its ranks, disregarding the input of sister churches, will in the end compromise not only her integrity but the integrity of us all. Pastors and staff must continually battle the temptation to bring in new members with little, if any, interaction with the church the candidate is leaving. Leadership cannot disregard this component of the transfer process for the sake of mere growth.

Before we leave this topic, let's admit that some churches enjoy the notoriety of being liberal, especially in areas of morality. In other words, they relish the reputation that turns a blind eye to the lifestyles of its members. They see this liberality as faddish and hip. Remember that Paul faced the same struggle with church members in Corinth who may have enjoyed their reputation for tolerance of loose-living members. Paul was more shocked by the indifference of the congregation than he was by the actual member's incestuous relationship. Sad to say, many of today's churches evidence much of the same spirit: winking at the flagrant, public sin of its members while enjoying the notoriety of the community. I once heard a preacher say, "The church has gotten used to the dark." By this he meant that the church has accommodated herself to her environment and lolled into passivity. Churches are no longer embarrassed by immoral behavior but see tolerance to such behavior as an admirable trait. Of course, on the other side, churches that stress a more stringent biblical view are seen as strict, judgmental, or void of grace. Naturally, the public gravitates toward those congregations who will make allowances for unbiblical behavior.

I often wonder how some churches grow without any drop in attendance, without hitting a glitch. Perhaps they have discovered a manner of discipleship that slips by the hard sayings of Christ without dropping numbers. Wow! If only Jesus had known their method, it could have saved him much in the way of heartache—just kidding!

Help for the Laity:
You Must Be Committed to Biblical Membership

Churches that implement a stronger, more well-defined membership process will face much in the way of difficulty. And without the support of the laity, most of these churches won't survive the very changes they implement. Congregations will then quickly lapse into an apathetic attitude toward membership in general, which means that the procedure itself will return to being little more than a move from one country club to another. If the laity does not value the integrity of church membership, both individually and corporately, then there is little chance that the leadership will survive the opposition that is certain to come.

You cannot sit on the sideline of this issue. I believe it is paramount to the church in America. This means that you need to voice your support for the leadership on the front line of these changes. Laity cannot back down halfway into the process. Churches will be called upon to examine and possibly change their by-laws and constitutions. They must determine if their present governmental structure is biblically sound and adequate to correct flagrant abuse of membership as well as "transfer of membership." If, after prayer and Bible study, this is evident, they must proceed. Let me warn you: this gets painful when those in positions of leadership are forced to confront the lifestyles of family members and close friends.

Laity who do not respect or grasp the importance of this area of church government will be of no help when the leadership comes under fire. This is why no pastor or church leader should attempt this without spending much time in prayer, study, and then bringing the congregation to a level of biblical understanding prior to the church changing its present practice. Laity should also make a public commitment to the process, recognizing the difficulty of the adjustments. Again, this is to be done with mercy and grace. No laity should be enlisted to serve on a committee that have not first been screened extensively.

CHAPTER 11

Confrontation: Do I Have the Right?

AVE YOU EVER WANTED TO whip your neighbor's kids or correct another man's wife or a friend's husband? Have you ever wished you could tell your boss to sit down and let you make some changes in the company? Have you sat in a congregation recently and thought, *Boy, I'd like to tell these people a thing or two*? May I ask you a question? *What stopped you?* Why didn't you just grab a belt, speak your mind, and make that correction or preach that sermon?

I can read your thoughts: *Because I didn't have that right.* In other words, you are saying, "I lacked the jurisdiction." Jurisdiction has to do with one's area of authority, the boundaries or parameters by which a person or organization can exercise authority.

In fact, the word *jurisdiction* is critical to our discussion and to the congregation's understanding of church government. For example, members who are living contrary to the Scripture might look at you and say, "What right do you have to correct me?" or, more bluntly, "Mind your own business." Imagine a small child making such a declaration to its parent. Church leadership as well as laity are often intimidated by such remarks, cowering from any form of confrontation. But think about it. Do the local church and its leaders have a right to invade the private lives of members and demand accountability? Does the church have jurisdiction over those who claim membership?

First, before we can answer the question, we must understand jurisdiction. For example, I do not discipline my neighbor's children. Why? Because they are not mine. They are not under my authority—an authority, I might add, that is recognized by both God and the government. I am only responsible for those with whom I have been entrusted. I am accountable to God and the government to see that those who are under my roof grow to be respectable adults. To disregard this obligation is a criminal offense in both courts.

Yet how many churches are raising delinquent members, spiritual children who are in fact a detriment to society? These are rebel members who tell church leaders, "It's none of your business." They show the leadership the door, while letting them know, "You have no jurisdiction here." But is that true? Does the church have authority in the lives of its parishioners? Has today's leadership relinquished territory, allowing members to join with little, if any, counsel as to the church's jurisdiction in their lives? Have we short-circuited a golden opportunity to address habitual, public disobedience by our failure to teach and grasp this idea of jurisdiction? Beyond this, how do members feel when we steer clear of their rebellious lifestyles?

I remember, on one occasion, my oldest daughter backing out of the driveway to meet some friends. I had followed her out to the car with the standard list of questions. *Who are you going with? Where are you going? How long will you be gone?* It was then that I noticed tears in her eyes. Thinking that I had upset her with my barrage of questions, I began to apologize. She responded, "Thanks, Dad, for caring." My concern demonstrated to her a real love, which she later confided was not necessarily present in the lives of her friends. The tragedy of today's church is that too many members are running loose with no one asking any questions at all. Keep in mind that if I neglect the discipline of my own children I am not only guilty of a criminal offense but of something worse; I communicate a lack of love. The same is true of the family of God. Remember our judge from a previous chapter, who reminded the father that his child was a minor under the father's authority, which therefore made the father liable.

While on vacation I thought it rather amusing that the local golf course monitored my behavior more closely than the average church would have. They were adamant that I behave on the course in a way that was consistent with the reputation of both the club and the sport. I understood that if my behavior were to become less than gentlemanly, I would be asked to leave. Why? Because once I stepped on their course, they had jurisdiction. Isn't it interesting that every organization, from the country club to the Boy Scouts, has some code of conduct in order for a person to be a member in good standing? Such organizations even go so far as to exercise that jurisdiction, while the local church recoils at such a thought.

Jurisdiction means "the right of authority," and it determines the right to invade people's lives. Simply put, jurisdiction is the right to give advice, provide input, and even monitor a person's behavior. Keep in mind that, according to the government and the Word of God, I have a right and an obligation to exercise control over my children. This means that I can intervene with correction and discipline in their lives. In the case of my own children, this is easy because they are mine.

But what about the average church member? What warrants my right to invade the life of another and claim jurisdiction? The answer is *identity*. For example, my children identify themselves as mine, and they reinforce that by including my last name as a part of theirs. So, in light of our discussion, what about those who call themselves "Christian"?

The Critical Issue of Identity

One of the first complete sentences I sought to learn as a missionary in Africa was, "Are you a Christian?" Once I had mastered these three Shona words, "*muri muchristu here*," I was on the move. Every day in the *musika* (market), I hounded shoppers with "Muri muchristu here?" However, as much as I enjoyed my new linguistic gift, it was short-lived. A local African pastor explained that most nationals would respond with *hongu* (yes) as a cultural nicety. Church leaders reminded me that the locals wanted to please me. So back to the language tutor

I went, seeking to develop other ways to confront people about their salvation.

But I never fully surrendered my straightforward, no-nonsense question. For me, it was a matter of establishing identity; I needed to know. Why? Because most of my interaction with people is based on either speaking to them about their salvation or fellowshipping with them around the faith. Identity is critical to believers; we put a fish on the back of our cars, we hang a cross around our neck, and we use a variety of emblems to identify ourselves. What does this have to do with our discussion on confrontation? Let me illustrate.

Suppose you go to a school play where the four year olds are all dressed in khaki pants or skirts, white shirts or blouses, and paper-sack masks pulled over their heads to conceal their identities. You and the other parents are watching as the little tikes go through their song and dance. Suddenly you notice one child becoming very disruptive, slapping the others and just being a general menace. As you study the child, you become more and more convinced that the little prodigal is yours. So you march up on stage in the middle of the production and snatch the sack from the child's head, only to discover that the shocked little face staring back at you is not yours. Now, let me ask you, what would be your response?

Naturally, your answer is "nothing." You would simply crawl back to your seat as quietly as possible, apologizing to the parents and thanking God that the rebel is not yours. You see, the issue of identity determined your reaction, your jurisdiction, and whether or not you could discipline. Remember, the only reason you went up on the stage was to correct bad behavior, and the only reason you didn't was because you had no right.

Now let's take this a step further. Suppose a new employee joins your firm. You introduce yourself, and during your break you have a pleasant conversation. In the course of your interaction, you ask if he is a Christian, to which he responds *yes*. However, over the course of several weeks, you hear profanity and witness such lewd behavior that you wonder whether he understood the question at all. Most of us would simply ignore the behavior and perhaps avoid the individual, speaking only when absolutely necessary and keeping our conversations as generic and brief as possible.

But let me ask you, *is this what God desires of us?* In fact, doesn't the Scripture demand the opposite? "My brothers, if one of you should wander from the truth and someone should bring him back, remember this: Whoever turns a sinner from the error of his way will save him from death and cover over a multitude of sins" (James 5:19–20 NIV). One might say, "It is not my place," but is that true? To think in such a way is the equivalent of a mother in the illustration above lifting the bag, seeing that it is her son, and returning to her seat. In fact, to do nothing at that point is far more damaging, because the mother not only knows that the disruptive child is hers but everyone in the auditorium knows it as well.

People must learn that a quick answer of "yes, I am a Christian" gives the church at large and its membership the right to question habitual, public, inappropriate behavior. Note the words *habitual*, *public*, and *inappropriate*. A word like *habitual* helps us to differentiate between a slip-up and a pattern. All of us understand the possibility of a fit of anger or saying or doing something that we know to be inappropriate. For example, the employee in the above illustration drops a wrench on his finger and lets out a four-letter word. You might think, *Okay, I might have done the same thing in the moment.* However, if the person uses profanity repeatedly, day after day, week after week with no sense of guilt, then confrontation should no longer be an option but rather a necessity. Why? Habitual disobedience is indicative of a much deeper problem, and if left to itself, it will threaten the mission of the church everywhere, including the workplace in question.

The myriads of people who so readily identify themselves with the body of Christ must understand the church's right to exercise jurisdiction. Some might ask: "Can we hold believers accountable who are outside one's local church?" In other words, "Do I have the right to correct behavior when the person is not a member of my church?" Whenever people identify themselves as Christian, it entitles others who share that title to expect a level of Christlike conduct that the general populace doesn't necessarily have to obey. You might want to read that sentence a second time.

I require a level of behavior out of my children that I cannot expect out of others. Why? My children are a part of my family and are therefore under my jurisdiction. In the same way, if I work in a company with an employee who claims to be a Christian and yet his behavior is barbaric, I have a right and even a biblical obligation to confront him. His conduct interferes with the great commission and weakens not only his testimony but also that of myself and Christians everywhere. Think about it. How often have you, when trying to share your faith, been reminded of the hypocrisy of professing Christians. If I am seeking to further the kingdom while a fellow employee is at the same time tearing it down, then we are essentially a house divided—a concept our enemy knows well. What you have just read is at the heart of fixing much of what's wrong in the church and in this nation.

Helping the Laity: Confrontation in the Public Arena

Every layperson reading this chapter understands the dynamics of the illustration above. For example, you work with someone who identifies himself or herself as a Christian. Yet the more you are around them, the more you question their Christianity. You see no evidence of a relationship with Christ. In fact, we are not talking about an occasional slip-up; we're talking about gross and habitual immorality. Worse yet is the damage done to those who you may be trying to influence others for Christ. You may think that to do nothing will only bring greater loss; but to address the problem may result in misunderstanding and possibly even termination.

Think for a moment, though, about the repercussions if you choose to be quiet. Doesn't your silence communicate apathy and indifference? In other words, won't those fellow employees who don't hold to your beliefs see those beliefs as having little if any real value? In as kind and gracious a way as possible, is it not better to privately voice your concern over another's lifestyle? Doesn't it communicate a "family dynamic" and, moreover, a discipline of the faith? If he asks what right you have to question his behavior, isn't the answer "because we are part of the same family"?

You will most likely hear the words "judge not." I believe this verse is one of the most misunderstood in the Bible. Paul counseled the membership at Corinth with this: "It isn't my responsibility to judge outsiders, but it certainly is your responsibility to judge those inside the church who are sinning" (1 Corinthians 5:12 NLT). In other words, when the world counsels the church to "judge not," this is the equivalent of someone telling you—once you discover that the child under the paper sack is yours—to leave him alone. Voices in the crowd may shout, "You have no right to correct that child." You shout back, "I have every right. This child is mine." The world has been shouting a lot here lately when it comes to the church confronting her own family. Don't listen.

Confrontation: The Need for Radical Evangelism

Old Testament prophets, though compelled by God, were often faced with apathy and indifference, their message shrouded in a cloud of insurrection and insubordination. Their congregation was made up of masses who cared little for the urgency of the times, men and women who had been lulled into mindless sleep over the years. This slumberous existence grew deeper in response to the endless number of false prophets who saw it as their mission to quiet the cries of the alarmists—alarmists who would in time be discovered to have been mouthpieces of the Almighty. Heavenly cries were sent to wake up a nation of priests, and in the midst of enormous spiritual detachment, they went forth.

Jeremiah would strap on a yoke and march into religious gatherings with a warning to repent or perish. Isaiah would rip his garments off and streak through the town center, echoing much the same message. Prophets swallowed pride and raced across history with a "thus says the Lord." This form of confrontation, though compelling to some, was annoying to others. The religious communities of their day scoffed at such proceedings, while others shuddered. A few were frightened by the desperate measures these men went to in order to be heard. Their madness splashed across the face of a sleepy nation like a pail of ice water.

The church in America, including many pastors and church leaders, face similar circumstances. They are like a spaced-out, drugged congregant who sits in the pew, basking in state-of-the-art lighting, music, and video while slipping further down the road to eternity. Comfortably seated, surrounded by soft voices, they meander toward judgment, occasionally interrupted by the prophetic voice of truth.

Churches must reevaluate their programs and methodology if there is to be any repentance at all. Radical steps of evangelism must be utilized. Some actions are as simple as rummaging through old membership records, while others are as radical as a return to street preaching. Men and women will once again move through their neighborhoods, inviting people not to church but to Christ, and they will not leave a front door because someone gives a good answer; they will only walk away only after receiving the *right* answer. These are followers of Christ who are willing to ask their friends and neighbors about their *walk* rather than their church home.

Confrontational, no-nonsense evangelism perseveres through the uncomfortable moments, when "why don't you leave" is quietly introduced into the conversation. A confrontation of this kind causes the Old Testament patriarchs to lean over the banisters of heaven and smile at the similarity to their own radical ways. Radical? Not really. What would you do to save those you love from certain doom if you had been given ample warning? Let's be honest. It is not that we are embarrassed but rather that we no longer believe in doom coming at all. If "the just shall live by faith," then we might want to ask as Jesus did in Luke 18:8, "When the Son of Man comes, will he find faith on the earth?"

CHAPTER 12

Confrontation: Can It Work in the Local Church?

M Y WIFE AND I HAVE raised four children: two boys and two girls, the girls being the older and the boys the younger. Often, in the course of moving through airports as missionaries, we would divide our responsibilities, which meant that she would smile and say, "I've got the girls; you take the boys." Looking back, I think I got the bad end of the deal, because our boys were *all* boy. The principle was simple, though. All four children were ours, and we recognized that the distribution of supervision would ensure monitored behavior.

The church must understand, as did my wife and I did, that if accountability is to be practiced, then it must be distributed among officers such as pastor, elders, and deacons. This will also ensure that the pastor is not the Lone Ranger. Why is this important? Churches and Christians that choose to exercise the biblical principles of confrontation will eventually run into the problem of how to implement such a plan. Let's face it: most churches have resident memberships that are bulky and cumbersome. Some members are so lost in the system that the FBI would have difficulty locating them. And if this is not bad enough, churches have the added weight of nonresident memberships, where only God only knows (and He does) who and where they are. So, once a church has determined to implement measures toward greater responsibility for her members, how can it do so and still maintain a level of accountability?

One answer, and perhaps the easiest, is for churches to incorporate into the curriculum of age-graded Sunday Schools or small groups a better grasp of accountability when it comes to individual members' behavior. Teachers and lay leaders must recognize their responsibility to address repeated, unbiblical conduct that could reflect poorly upon the greater body of believers. Again, remember that this is behavior that is contrary to Scripture and is lived out publicly and has become a way of life. The church must teach lay leadership, as well as the general membership, the discipline of confrontation and the correct way to carry it out.

Churches, regardless of size, that have aggressively broken down the membership into smaller entities will be better suited to confront and discipline. Why? Because their resident members have been assigned to appropriate, age-graded classes or have been enrolled in small groups of some sort. Remember, it is paramount that churches take strong measures to ensure that every member is enrolled in something. This will delegate the monitoring of the membership to more manageable groups and can be especially helpful to the leadership who may feel too misinformed to approach a parishioner. Again, it is important for pastors and staff to incorporate the topic of accountability into their discipleship curriculum. If the task is shared among smaller entities, you will be much more able to address spasmodic attendance and rumored habitual and public misconduct. I am convinced that few churches know all their members' names, let alone how they live. That is a sin. Again, these manageable units will increase the church's ability to oversee its membership.

Critical at this point is adequate training of all leadership. Pastors can't read this book and railroad ahead with an agenda of confrontation without training others. Staff, Sunday School teachers, and small group leaders, as well as all other leaders, should understand that the primary motive for small groups is not merely the dispersing of information but also to maintain accountability. By *accountability* I mean, making every effort to keep up with how the membership is progressing in their spiritual walk and how they are living in relation to the tenets of Scripture. I can't say it enough: leadership at every level must be trained and equipped to carry out this function of the church. They must grasp the importance of accountability, and there can be no accountability without confrontation.

If there is a danger in the mega church, it is the difficulty of controlling large blocks of constituents who may choose not to join smaller organizational structures. For example, they join the church but nothing more. An article in *Christianity Today*, "Fixing Church Discipline," states, "It's tempting to finger the mega-church as the prime suspect, if only for its size. In such settings, it is hard to keep track of the membership rolls, let alone member's personal lives. Congregants from the 9:30 service rarely meet those who attend the 11:00 service, even if they may be committed to biblical mandates to help a fellow church member in spiritual or moral trouble. But how can one even tell a member? Many people attending these churches may be church hoppers or perennial visitors, considering themselves free-floating Christians without accountability—and they like it that way" (Jeschke, 2005, 30).

This sheds light on why a number of mega-church members see their involvement as a peripheral issue. In other words, they can claim church affiliation and yet see an active role as insignificant. And if larger churches refuse to address the issue, then they begin to resemble a man who is happy to bring children into the world but who refuses to be involved in their upbringing; his children are allowed to roam the streets without accountability. This is not to single out the large church, for there are numerous examples of mega churches that have incorporated extensive checks and balances in monitoring their membership. However, larger churches must recognize a greater struggle in maintaining their membership if they are not quickly assimilated into a small-group setting.

A good deterrent is "new member orientation," which should be a requirement, and the last session should end with an introduction to a particular small group leader. This is not merely giving a new member a list of small groups available to them; rather it involves introducing him to one person who will maintain contact. It is true that we cannot make a member participate in small groups, but we *can* assign a spiritually mature believer to come alongside the new inductee and provide both support and accountability. People who refuse such identification might be telling us something about their future aspirations. Churches must understand that the initial entry process (salvation or transfer of membership) is the golden opportunity to initiate whatever requirements the church deems necessary.

Helping the Laity: Small Group Leaders and a New Mandate

If you are reading this and at the same time holding some teaching position, then you are either a part of the solution or a part of the problem. You must understand the importance of your role as a leader. In essence, you are the front line of hope for the church by your commitment to confronting members who are, by their lifestyles, killing the church. Every name on your roll is either helping or harming the Great Commission by whether or not they are living within the guidelines of Scripture. If you refuse to be responsible for the lives entrusted to your care, and instead you remain neutral, then you will be accountable to a holy God. Does that sound strong? It should. However, let me also warn you: do not proceed without proper training and guidance from your pastor and leadership. The next chapter is critical as to how we should proceed.

Those who may not be in a position of leadership are not exempt from involvement. Every believer is a part of the family of God and is therefore responsible for all others within the family. Identity as a believer gives each one the right to, in a scriptural fashion, address the behavior of another, regardless of church affiliation. Once you have determined a person's Christian identity, it is within reason to approach him about unbiblical behavior. This should only be done according to Scripture and after personal observation. This should never be done based on hearsay and innuendo. Further, confrontation is not to be done in public to avoid embarrassing the person, nor is it to be done apart from any motive other than that of *love*.

Coach Wooden said this about confronting someone.

> I never wanted to embarrass or humiliate. The purpose of criticism or discipline is to correct, enhance, educate, modify behavior, or bring about a positive change. It takes great skill to do so without incurring ill feelings, animosity, anger, or even hatred. A leader who lacks the skills necessary in this area will often see his or her attempt to offer constructive criticism reduced to destructive criticism. You will have damaged your own team by making one or more of its members less effective. In providing criticism, you must not open wounds that are slow to heal. An individual subjected to personal insults, especially in front of others, can be needlessly impaired. (Wooden and Jamison, 2005, 172)

Even as I read Wooden's response, I think to myself, *No one has to explain to him his role as a coach.* He understands that his task of guiding young men to be the best they can be is laced through and through with confrontation. Neither a player or nor a spectator would expect anything less.

CHAPTER 13

Confrontation: Getting the Facts Straight

A NYONE WHO ENJOYS A MYSTERY understands the initials "PI." *PI* means "private investigator." For most churches and leadership, the thought of intervening in the lives of its membership, regardless of the scriptural mandate, is frightening. Why? Let's admit that most of us are afraid of invading people's privacy for fear that we sound like a detective rather than a sibling in Christ.

Private investigation should mean just that: keeping the matter private. Jesus said, "If your brother sins against you, go and show him his fault, *just between the two of you*. If he listens to you, you have won your brother over. But if he will not listen, take one or two others along, so that every matter may be established by the testimony of two or three witnesses. If he refuses to listen to them, tell it to the church, treat him as you would a pagan or a tax collector" (Matthew 18:15–17 NIV, emphasis mine). We get the feeling as Christ walks his followers through the process that it is to be done discretely: in other words, with as few people knowing as possible. Wiersbe states, "Approach the person who sinned and speak with him alone ... go to him with the idea of winning your brother, not winning an argument" (Wiersbe, 1980, 127).

This is good exegesis. It is not a matter of walking away from a confrontation and gloating over our persuasive abilities; it is a matter of knowing in our hearts that a brother has been salvaged. As we saw earlier, our goal is *transformation*, not *alienation*. But let's admit it; this is not easy. MacArthur stresses the word *reprove* and suggests that "the brother is to be shown his sin in such a way that he cannot escape recognizing it for what it is" (MacArthur, 1984, 128). The confronting believer is taking the Word of God, not as a machete hacking the way through a forest but rather as a scalpel in the hands of a surgeon removing a cancerous tumor.

Note how Jesus continues the progression. "But if he will not listen, take one or two others along." Wiersbe further comments on the need for "assisting in prayer and persuasion, but also to serve as witnesses, if the matter is brought before the church as to the truth of the conversation" (Wiersbe, 1980, 127). Jesus is stressing that the undertaking be done quietly and with as few people knowing as possible. When confession is necessary, it should be carried out only to the degree that it is known. This is to protect both the reputation of the person and the church. Only an unrepentant member who refuses the first two attempts at private consultation should be taken before the whole church. Warning: when it comes to formal public discipline, there should be at least two witnesses who have seen the offense. If they cannot be found, then the matter is to be dropped. Remember that confrontation is the preface to church discipline and should be done privately, protecting all parties involved as well as the testimony and witness of the church.

Before we leave this passage, I want to mention two words that caught my attention: "your brother." Notice that Christ makes it clear that the offender is to be treated as a member of the body of believers, regardless of what we might think. He should be handled as you would handle your own family. In the case of those who were causing discord at Thessalonica, Paul counseled the church at large: "If anyone does not obey our instruction in this letter, take special note of him. Do not associate with him, in order that he may feel ashamed. Yet do not regard him as an enemy, but warn him as a brother" (2 Thessalonians 3:14–15 NIV). Note that Paul says, "Do not regard him as an enemy, but warn him as a brother." People often approach one another after simmering over the issue for a while, angrily rehearsing what they will say. They confront with a less than Christlike spirit and thereby do extensive damage to the cause of Christ in the workplace or some other environment where the lost are watching. Keep in mind that the person being confronted is to be treated as a family member, but let me also add that nonbelievers cannot intimidate the church into doing nothing.

PI should also stand for "personal integrity." Probably no single factor threatens this church chore more than the feeling of one's own unworthiness. While there is no one perfect to whom this task may be assigned, confronters must be men and women of impeccable character. In other words, they must demonstrate a level of integrity that is above reproach. Usually, when one makes such a statement, there is an immediate response: "Who then can carry out such a requirement?"

Paul alludes to this in Galatians. "Brothers, if someone is caught in a sin, you who are spiritual should restore him gently. But watch yourself, or you also may be tempted. Carry each other's burdens, and in this way you will fulfill the law of Christ" (Galatians 6:1–2 NIV). Notice that restoration and confrontation is to be done by "you who are spiritual." The implication is that the process is to be accomplished by members within the body who are walking in the Spirit and are being led as such.

Derek Thomas believes that "Paul is referring back to those in chapter five who were displaying the Fruits of the Spirit ... These were not walking after the flesh but in step with the Spirit" (Thomas, 2004, 147). This is the quality of member who exemplifies the "mind of Christ" and is careful to note all the requirements listed in Galatians 6:1.

Dr. Norman Maclean tells of an incident in which a teacher had given her class the assignment of memorizing a clause from the Apostle's Creed. On the following morning, the first boy began, "I believe in God the Father Almighty, Maker of heaven and earth." The second boy said, "I believe in Jesus Christ his only Son our Lord." The recitation went on until it reached the point where one of the boys said: "From thence he shall come to judge the quick and the dead." Then there fell a silence until finally the next boy in line said to the examiner, "Please, sir, the boy who believes in the Holy Ghost is absent today" (Rees, 1969, 127–128).

May God help us to seek out men and women who believe and are filled with the Holy Spirit and are most respected within the body of believers. Beyond this, may they remember the words of Frances A. Schaffer: "To be a Bible-believing Christian demands humility regarding others in the body of Christ."

Helping the Laity: Being a Good Private Investigator

The process of confrontation done in an unbiblical fashion will do much damage to the Great Commission. Now, take a moment and copy that sentence. Then tape it to your forehead and practice what you will say when you go and confront this person. Every component of this chapter is relevant to the laity. The matter is not to be a source of gossip at the water cooler, nor is it to be done with secondhand information. Adequate private investigation will result in a level of integrity that may not only win the person being confronted but also serve as a stimulus to dialogue with others. Again, as I said in a pervious chapter, if you enjoy cutting the switch, you are not qualified.

We must also listen. Larry King said, "I never learned anything while I was talking" (King, 2011, 130). Those who confront must above all else learn to *listen*. As James said, "Be quick to listen and slow to speak."

Again, you should not initiate confrontation without being filled with the Holy Spirit. Paul identifies confronters as "you which are spiritual," meaning "you who are under the control of the Spirit of Christ." To attempt to confront without exercising the humility and grace of Christ is to possibly do irreparable damage to the mission of the church. You must determine if you are presently walking with Christ in every area of your life, seeking as best you can to live within the tenets of Scripture—before you set out to do anything. You cannot go, as my mom used to say, "half-cocked." Undoubtedly, she was referring to the position of a trigger on a gun. In such a position, a believer will say and do things they will later regret. Actress Janet Leigh said, "John Wayne once said something that I thought was funny. He said, 'I'm not an actor, I'm a reactor.'" We must constantly fight the urge to react. Confrontation is not reacting to people but rather carrying out a command of Scripture. To react is to go with emotions that will most likely result in hurt feelings and alienation (Fagen, 2006, 256).

CHAPTER 14

Grace Break: A Story to Illustrate

"**W**ORLDLY WOMAN" THE LOCALS CALLED her. Sarah had managed to sleep with half the men in the community since her husband had died twelve years earlier. At least it had kept a roof over her head and loneliness from her heart. But someone had squealed and blown her cover, and now, here were the Pharisees, pulling her by the hair and cursing because God hadn't made hair strong enough to drag a body.

Her cohorts called her "lucky" but not today. They hid in the alley, watching from a safe distance, thanking God it wasn't them. Strange, it was only yesterday that they had been bragging, "Lucky, you can pull a trick right under their noses" as they nodded toward the temple and giggled, knowing that the zealots would come later in the evening, rough them up, curse, swear, and take care of business. But they paid good money, and that was all that mattered.

"Let's see what the rabbi from Nazareth does with you," said one of her captors. Both wrists ached as two temple guards yanked and dragged her as if she were a dead animal being hauled to the dump.

Her mind raced to a good memory. That was a reaction she did well, mostly when men were cruel. She thought about her mother saying, "You're going to be something special. I just know it." Then she would smile and pull Sarah close and give her hug. Sarah was thankful her mother hadn't lived to see this day. The voices stopped until the one who pulled the hardest growled, "Well, teacher." Everyone was quiet, and a couple of women whispered, but only for a moment. "You know the Law. She was caught in the act. Now what do you say we do with the little—" He stopped as children pressed in closer.

Sarah tried to pull her robe down, embarrassed as a dark-eyed little girl pointed and then hid. "Well," said her accusers, exaggerating the single syllable, pulling the word in a mocking way. "Shall we?" The leader tossed a stone at the feet of the teacher. Sarah reached a hand to her left eye and wiped the blood that trickled down her cheek like tears.

The teacher grew still, but the wind didn't. It wanted to answer. Time seemed to stop, waiting on the teacher's answer as if uncertain whether it should continue if he didn't. Finally, he did, and his voice was calm, slow, and tender.

"You," the word dangled in eternity, looking for a place to rest. "Without." At this he began to write, his finger brushing the dust, names coming up out of the dirt as if they had always been there. The wind ceased as if it were in on it.

"You without sin, cast the first stone." With each stroke, another official moved back, slipping into the crowd. The older ones took their stones, not wanting to leave any evidence. Jesus still didn't look up. He toyed with the dust, his voice just above a whisper. "Where are your accusers?"

She sat up. "There are ..." She scanned the crowd. "There are none." The teacher continued to kneel, refusing to join the crowd that still lingered, gaping at her.

"Neither do I accuse you." He looked not *at* her but *into* her and smiled. She'd had few smile at her before, even men who sought her services would never do that. Most in the city only showed their disapproval—at least publicly—shaking their heads from side to side, making sure that everybody could see.

He stood, reached out his hand, lifted her to her feet, and waited for her to look at him. "Now go and sin no more." The crowd parted like the Red Sea as she started to walk away. She went ten steps—she counted them—and then turned and watched him with his rock, tossing it in the air like a kid with a ball, going right on with his teaching. For the first time in twelve years, she smiled too. Her eyes danced with the rock as he talked of his Father's love.

This story is a reminder that to attempt to confront with any spirit other than that of Christ is detrimental to the intent of Scripture.

Helping the Laity: A Picture of Grace

No story better exemplifies the picture of confrontation. We see Jesus effectively dealing with this woman without embarrassing her. He addresses her sin without destroying her in the process. In fact, everyone would do well to read this story several times prior to confronting another follower of Christ.

CHAPTER 15

Confrontation Is Commanded

LEONARDO DA VINCI SAID, "HE who does not punish evil commands it to be done." Da Vinci was right, but let me expand the thought. When we ignore evil, we are strengthening its hold on our lives and those we love. Confrontation must never be seen as just an option for the more fanatical; it is to be recognized as a deterrent to evil. The nature of God, his Son, his messengers, his Word, and his people are all confrontational. To say otherwise is to fail to recognize the very heart of our Creator. Three words are paramount and must be voiced often: *confrontation is commanded.*

In our early courting days, my wife would always sign her notes with "Shiela, lest you forget." Well, just to let you know, I haven't forgotten. But with that said, let me go ahead and warn you that this section is more pastoral in nature. In other words, unless you are a preacher preparing a message, you may find this information somewhat technical.

The book of James, written by the head of the church at Jerusalem and the half-brother of Jesus, is perhaps the most practical book in the New Testament. It is interesting that this letter closes with a "lest you forget" appendage: "My brothers, if one of you should wander from the truth and someone should bring him back, remember this: Whoever turns a sinner from the error of his way will save him from death and cover over a multitude of sins" (James 5:19–20). James, the overseer of the early church, cautioned the leadership not to forget but to watch out for those who might wander off.

I don't believe this was an afterthought by the Holy Spirit but rather a critical caution. James ended his epistle with a clear admonition to the body of believers to maintain a high level of accountability. He spoke to the church of the importance of "watch care" and proposed a hypothetical situation, a strong possibility that sooner or later the family of God would face a prodigal. The phrase "one of you" included all of the very recipients who would hear the letter read. I like D. Edmond Hiebert's comments on the word translated *wander*. He suggested that this is the "familiar metaphor of a sheep nibbling the grass among the rocks and crags … moving farther and farther away from the security and safety of the shepherd and the flock. The aorist tense denotes an occasional rather than a habitual occurrence. The verb may be interpreted as either passive or middle in force. If passive, the person is led by another, deceived, tricked, coerced into disobedience. But if in the middle case then 'he went off on his own'" (Heibert, 1979, 307).

You may not think the aorist tense is important (passive or middle), but how one leaves the fellowship of the church is critical in determining how he is to be confronted. For example, was it a willful, rebellious, defiant act? Or was it gradual, more like a child pulled by the tide of the sea. Regardless of how you interpret the grammar, the thought is clear: wanderers must be rescued. In fact, this responsibility of the church—and more so of the pastor—is paramount to the health and well-being of us all.

James was adamant; we must go after the wanderer. The Bible commands us to go and bring them back. James continued, saying that the one who initiates this redemptive process is not necessarily a minister or, for that matter, a leader, but is rather a "someone." In other words, this person does not have to possess a list of credentials but needs only a single attribute mentioned in Galatians 6:1: "you who are spiritual." This is a Spirit-filled follower of Christ who moves into the path of the wanderer and turns him around.

This could be like a layman friend of mine who was so nervous about his pastor's relationship with a female church member that he was willing to confront, even at the risk of being wrong. He admitted later, "Though my pastor was innocent at the time, I do believe that had I not intervened it would have progressed into something far more damaging." In other words, he believed that his pastor was nibbling grass, steadily moving into a pasture of heartache and ruin. It took a lot of courage on his part to address a camaraderie bordering on scandal.

Yet the truth is that we need more laity who are willing to be ostracized by their spiritual leaders for the sake of integrity. We need normal, everyday believers who refuse to sit silent while the enemy works his wiles in the body, seducing the saints, luring them into compromising positions. I love what F. LaGard Smith said in his book, *Fallen Shepherds Scattered Sheep.* "We are still our brother's keeper, even if he is our leader" (Smith, 1988, 26). Smith goes on to conclude, "Why do spiritual leaders fall? Because we deceive them about their own humanity. We let them think they walk on water and then act surprised when they drown" (Smith, 1988, 46). James was challenging—no, he was *commanding*—the early church to go after those who wander from the flock, because when leaders or laity are allowed to stray away from the body of believers into disobedience, then we all suffer.

Bill Hybels shares a heart-wrenching story in his book, *Courageous Leadership.*

> I'll never forget the breakfast I once had with a famous pastor who had wound up in a moral ditch. My only agenda was to be a brother to him and to let him know that he still mattered to God. That morning as we sat across from each other in the restaurant, I asked, "How are you supporting your family?"
>
> "Well," he shrugged, his voice full of sadness, "the family left, you know."
>
> "Oh, I'm so sorry. I didn't know," I said quietly. "Then, how are you supporting yourself these days?"

He tried to form the words, but they kept getting stuck in his throat. Finally he sighed and said, "I'm selling shoes," after which he buried his face in his hands and began to sob.

After he regained his control of his emotions, he recounted a whole list of modifications he should have incorporated into his life that would likely have led to a totally different outcome. What made his pain even deeper that morning was knowing that he had considered making some of those changes years ago, but he hadn't done it." (Hybels, 2002, 237–8)

As I read this I thought of the countless number of mistakes made by men of God who fail to bring "voices of truth" into their lives, those Nathans we invite into our lives to keep watch over our wandering and to wake us up, if need be. Too many pastors and their families are strewn along the highway of ministry because no one could confront them. Either pastors isolate themselves from others or others refuse to confront them because of who they are. Regardless, the cost to the church is excruciating.

Recently I was in a theater, watching one of those movies where the suspense is building and your hero is in jeopardy. At any moment, I knew that someone was going to jump out and cause every grown man in the room to scream like a girl. Sorry, but I'm the guy who jumps and shouts a warning thirty seconds before it happens. The tragedy of believers is that we are often more apt to shout in a theater, warning our favorite movie star in a make-believe world than we are a fellow believer who is in real spiritual danger. As D. Edmond Hiebert states in his commentary on James, "It must be the concern of all believers" (Hiebert, 1979, 333). He goes on to quote R. V. G. Tasker: "There is something fatally wrong about us if we have no strong desire to bring back sinners to God" (Hiebert, 1979, 333). Perhaps Tasker is right, if the membership of a local church can stand by and watch the current of the world catapult one life after another over a cliff. Members observe comrades, and even their leaders, drifting to their doom, and yet they refuse to throw a rope. Again, James states, "Remember this: Whoever turns a sinner from the error of his way will save him from death and cover a multitude of sins" (James 5:20 NIV). Confrontation is commanded.

Believers today must grasp the significance of this biblical mandate and the importance to all involved. To the confronter, it is an act of obedience. To the rebel, it is a splash of cold water and one that may wake him up from a game of religious roulette. In essence, it may save his life. As we saw in James 5, "Remember this: Whoever turns a sinner from the error of his way will save him from death." James uses strong imperatives: "Remember this"; "Don't forget this"; "Keep this foremost in your thoughts." Remember what? Remember that you are possibly saving someone from a premature death, and never forget that this is sin's natural progression. Beyond this, "you cover a multitude of sins."

This plea comes at the close of a letter viewed by many as a New Testament type of the book of Proverbs. James dogged the steps of young, new believers with practical advice and strong warnings, much like my questioning of my oldest daughter when she was backing out of the driveway. Like a lawyer delivering his closing arguments, James pleaded for the church not to forget those who strayed. He begged the leadership to go beyond salvation to continually carry out rescue operations. They were to join the front line of spiritual conflict, snatching from the enemy his most valuable tool: a backslider. We saw earlier that if any appendage of the body is left untreated, it will reek of decay and affect the entire body. Like a cancer, it will, if given time, infect the healthy tissue.

Does Scripture command such rescues? Yes. Is it tough to do? Yes. Simon Kistemaker states, "Tactfully reproving a person who is wandering from the truth is one of the most difficult tasks in the work of the church" (Kistemaker, 1987, 183). But remember that obedience to the Scripture is not a choice but rather a mandate for leadership and laity alike. Kistemaker goes on to caution, "If we fail to warn or speak out, we ourselves are guilty, for God holds us responsible. Yes, we are our brother's keeper."

Old Testament prophets were continually in the heat of this battle "to turn a sinner from the error of his ways." Ezekiel is a good example of James 5:19–20. He was commanded by God to preach repentance to the southern kingdom of Judah—in other words, to confront. However, because of his hesitancy, God reminded him of the severity of punishment if he chose to neglect the task. "Son of man, I have made you a watchman for the house of Israel; so hear the word I speak and give them warning from me. When I say to a wicked man, 'You will surely die,' and you do not warn him or speak out to dissuade him from his evil ways in order to save his life, that wicked man will die for his sin, and I will hold you accountable for his blood. But if you do warn the wicked man and he does not turn from his wickedness or from his evil ways, he will die for his sin; but you will have saved yourself" (Ezekiel 3:17–19 NIV).

In this case, the nation of Israel was wandering away, and it was Ezekiel to whom God would give the task of being the "watchman" or "confronter." Perhaps it would be good for pastors to preach and exegete Ezekiel 3:17–19 to their congregations, because we have all been called to be watchmen, and to disregard this divine mandate is a criminal act. If members are allowed to live outside the authority of Scripture without any form of confrontation, then, given enough time, we will have a crisis. And so we do.

By now you should be convinced that the role of confrontation in the ministry of the local church is a biblically based responsibility. However, confrontation is not always a "get in your face" type of event. Once you've made someone aware of a wrong, additional confrontations may not be necessary. This was illustrated in our earlier example of a fellow employee who claimed to be a Christian but whose actions spoke otherwise.

So, what does a believer do when all attempts fail and the person continues to live in defiance? In his book, *Dynamics of Spiritual Life: An Evangelical Theology of Renewal*, Richard Lovelace states:

There are a number of texts in the New Testament which counsel separation from those who are apparently inside the Christian fold, either because of moral delinquency of some kind (1 Cor. 5:11; 2 Thess. 3:6, 14) or because of false teaching (Rom. 16:17; Titus3:8–11). But in these instances the separation Paul enjoins has nothing to do with removal from church structures (either of the guilty party or of a righteous minority) but rather is a matter of shunning, of breaking off intimate fellowship with the offending party. Even in these cases, Paul is not counseling absolute loss of contact with the person punished, since he commands fraternal exhortation in both moral and doctrinal cases of discipline (2 Cor. 2:6–7; 2 Tim. 2:24–26). (Lovelace, 1979, 304)

Lovelace sees this as a biblical mandate but not one that requires continual confrontation. Instead, it may develop into something as simple as avoiding the person for a period of time. For example, Paul warns the entire church at Thessalonica, "to keep away from every brother who is idle and *does not live according to the teaching* you received from us" (2 Thessalonians 3:6, emphasis mine).

Knute Larson notes:

In matters of discipline Paul sometimes commanded ostracizing the offending person in order to produce a shame leading to repentance (1 Cor. 5:5, 11). The members of the assembly were to withdraw fellowship so the person would feel the consequences of his action. These consequences would prove the individual's heart. He would either repent or display prideful indifference. The command was also to be carried out for "every brother," removing the possibility of favoritism or misuse. Paul also recognized that this offending person would remain a brother, a member of the community of believers. He did not call for excommunication. Paul initiated a disciplinary measure in order to keep the church orderly and to maintain its good reputation. His purpose was to restore the brother. (Larson, 2000, 126–127)

The critical issue is the safeguarding of the reputation of the church while, as James stressed, salvaging the brother. Again, the goal of the church is to *convict*, not to *condemn*. Is this easy? Not necessarily. The body of believers will always walk a tightrope, balancing confrontation in one hand and compassion in the other. James 5:19–20 says, "My dear brothers and sisters, if anyone among you wanders away from the truth and is brought back again, you can be sure that the one who brings that person back will save that sinner from death and bring about the forgiveness of many sins."

Note the terminology used: *convert, turn around, bring back.* Each phrase describes the process of restoring a fellowship that has been compromised. James instructs these early believers to go out and do what cowboys do on a cattle drive—head them off at the pass. He gives the mandate in the form of a hypothetical situation ("if anyone among you wanders away from the truth"), knowing full well that this is a reality and a painful truth in every church. He almost seems to shout from the pages: "Sooner or later, the cares of the world will tug at the best of us. It's coming. Get ready for it."

How could James be so sure? As we saw earlier, being prone to wander is a characteristic of man, a never-ending desire to stray away from what we know to be good. This is the tragedy of our lives, and given enough time, we will all say, "Been there, done that." Tragically, Peter had discovered this tendency in his own life when he debated with the Lord on the night of Jesus' betrayal: "But he replied, 'Lord, I am ready to go with you to prison and to death'" (Luke 22:33 NIV). Jesus disregarded his objections and instead reminded him, "Simon, Simon, Satan has asked to sift you as wheat. But I have prayed for you, Simon, that your faith may not fail. And when you have turned back, strengthen your brothers" (Luke 22: 31–32 NIV). The word used in "when you've turned back" is used only twice in the New Testament, here and in the passage we just examined in James.

The great need of the church is to develop a program to aggressively go after those who are wandering. Those weakened lives have moved away from the authority figures entrusted with their care. Churches need men and women who will serve on the head-them-off-at-the-pass committee, people who will go and meet these wanderers where they are and aggressively seek to bring them back. This is not a job for the fainthearted. When someone is drowning in sin, the danger is that the rescuer can be taken down by the one drowning.

I remember white-water rafting with a friend on the Zambezi River in Zimbabwe, Africa. During our journey we came upon a young woman who had been thrown from another raft and was now bobbing down the rapids, screaming for help. Our guide, though intent on saving her, warned my friend and me, who were stationed at the front, "Be careful. She's desperate and dangerous." By this he meant that she could pose a real threat to us. Ultimately, we pulled her to safety.

But our guide's counsel must be repeated by every pastor to those who are going after members who are out of the church and drowning in the world. To attempt to bring anyone back into the fold is to risk one's own spiritual health in the process. For many who wander from the church there is a newfound freedom, one that they would love to pass on to any would-be rescuers. Those who stay away long enough become convinced that this "foot in the world" is all right. Satan has duped the backslider, made a deal in the wilderness that compromise is acceptable. This person, though needing to be salvaged, is a real threat to the confronter. To send spiritually immature members or the untrained out to address the prodigal is to further magnify the problem. Only those of the deepest level of spiritual growth should be assigned this task.

Sometimes I think churches need a "Lost and Found," a place to take those who have wandered off, reuniting them to the fellowship of the Lord and the membership. One man in our church commented, "The longer you are away, the harder it is to come back." He was talking about the embarrassment of attending after such a long absence. He confessed, "It is excruciating." This is why it is so important for the head-them-off-at-the-pass committee to hand them off to a group of volunteers who, in an unobtrusive way, help to welcome and acclimate them back into the fellowship of the church by sticking close to them during their initial reentry. Pastors and leaders should also counsel the general congregation to avoid derogatory remarks, which, though meant to be humorous, are in reality very damaging. "Man, where have you been? Wow, I thought the roof was going to fall in. Hey, look who's back." I know you could add some more.

Once again, though, the greater problem for spiritual leaders is, as it was in Ezekiel's time, a tendency toward indifference.

> The word of the Lord came to me: "Son of man, prophesy against the shepherds of Israel; prophesy and say to them: 'This is what the sovereign Lord says: Woe to the shepherds of Israel who only take care of themselves! Should not shepherds take care of the flock? You eat the curds, clothe yourselves with the wool, and slaughter the choice animals, but you do not take care of the flock. You have not strengthened the weak or healed the sick or bound up the injured. *You have not brought back the strays or searched for the lost.* You have ruled them harshly and brutally. So they were scattered because there was no shepherd, and when they were scattered they became food for all the wild animals. My sheep wandered over all the wild mountains and on every high hill. They were scattered over the whole earth, and *no one searched or looked for them.*
>
> "'Therefore, you shepherds, hear the word of the Lord: As surely as I live, declares the Sovereign Lord, because my flock lacks a shepherd and so has been plundered, and has become food for all the wild animals, and *because my shepherds did not search for my flock* but cared for themselves rather than for my flock, therefore, O shepherds, hear the

word of the Lord: This is what the Sovereign Lord says: I am against the shepherds and will hold them accountable for my flock. I will remove them from tending the flock so that the shepherds can no longer feed themselves. I will rescue my flock from their mouths, and it will no longer be food for them.'" (Ezekiel 34:1–10 NIV, emphasis mine)

Note the words "have not brought back the strays or searched for the lost ... no one searched for them." This was a strong indictment in Ezekiel's day against those spiritual leaders who were complacent. Jewish strays were roaming enemy territory, vulnerable and open to attack, and yet the shepherds demonstrated little if any concern. Again, the stress is not on those who have strayed as much as it is on the leadership who seem not to care. No wonder Christ called men such as these "hirelings" and summed up his own ministry with the words: "For the Son of Man came to seek and to save what was lost" (Luke 19:10 NIV). God requires the same in the heart of both pastor and laity alike.

Tragically, the church is experiencing a fatal flaw, because so few show a desire to bring back sinners. Os Guinness states, "The problem is not that Christians have disappeared but that the Christian faith has become so deformed" (Guinness, 1993, 43). That deformity is no more clearly seen than in the indifference of the church when it comes to confronting sin and going after those who have left the fellowship. If the church is to return to her moorings, then the remnant must get back to the difficult task of *converting*, of turning back the wayward. Going into the world's domain and assertively reclaiming those who have become entangled in her web is critical to purity. These prodigals who have deserted the church, abused their freedom, and become entrenched in behavioral patterns will, over time, undermine Christ and his church, unless we make every attempt to reclaim them.

I am reminded of an incident in which one of my daughters was in a friendship that I knew to be unhealthy. In an attempt to address the relationship, I spent several sleepless nights, and finally one evening I brought the matter into a major confrontation that resulted in tears and separation. Though painful, the confrontation ended a dangerous friendship and rekindled fellowship with Dad. Was it easy? Absolutely not! Was it necessary? Yes!

Helping the Laity: Your Role Is Critical

I am convinced that this discipline of the church cannot be accomplished without you, the laity. The task is so overwhelming to the leadership that without trained church members coming alongside the pastor and staff, it will not be possible. However, as you read this section, keep in mind that you will either be a part of the problem or a part of the solution. In other words, you are either actively involved in a church or you have drifted away and have not attended your church in some time. If you are a part of the latter group, then let me encourage you to return to your church family. Don't wait on someone to come looking for you; rather, like the prodigal, return home.

Beyond this, you can be a decisive tool in confronting if you choose to do so. But again, keep in mind that you must be trained and equipped to do so. This can only happen when your leaders become concerned over the volume of inactive members and initiate a plan for enlistment and training of volunteers. Don't be offended when your training mostly addresses what not to say and do. Like our river guide in the earlier story, laity must be constantly warned as to the danger of this type of rescue operation. This is not for the fainthearted or spiritually weak. In fact, let me caution you not to go it alone. By that I mean that you should not venture into this mission without first consulting with your leadership, sharing with them your concern over a particular member and why you feel qualified to approach the person. Listen to their advice and seek their blessing. Your church staff may have additional information that you are not privy to.

Please, don't go with opinions and personal reflections but rather with a clear objective of reclaiming the member. This is not a let-me-tell-you-what-I-think conversation but rather a reference to what the Bible says. And this is not a Bible over the head but rather an opening up of the Word as two people sit side-by-side and grasp the meaning of the Scripture. It is taking the Scripture and applying it to the person's life at that moment. Don't be like the man who so wanted to help at the scene of an accident that he shoved a woman out of the way, claiming to have had a course in first aid. The woman stood and watched the man's pitiful efforts and then tapped him on the shoulder and said, "When you get to the part about calling the doctor—I'm already here" (Brinkley, 2011, 193). In other words, use the expertise of those around you.

Let me also add this: don't think this is always going to be a sweet exchange of thoughts. Often, as innocent and gentle as you may try to be, there will still be a level of defensiveness on the part of the one being confronted. It is very possible that you will be attacked in the beginning, regardless of the sincerity of your intentions. I have often found the initial contact with a person to be strained, yet over time the person returns, broken and repentant, willing to listen and thankful for your concern.

CHAPTER 16

Preaching That Confronts

MEN WHO SENSE A CALL to ministry—and more so, to that of preaching—will often ask about authority. One student asked it this way: "How do you get that *oomph* in your voice?" When speaking about the preaching passion of her late husband, Peter Marshall, Catherine Marshall wrote, "An Army officer, admittedly thoroughly pagan, came to church only out of respect to his host and hostess. He left (after hearing a sermon by Peter Marshall) saying, 'If I heard that preacher often, I'd have to change my way of life—that's all'" (Marshall, 1949, 12). It was clear that her husband's preaching would have consistently challenged the soldier's lifestyle until he changed it.

John A. Broadus says it well. "The very nature of the Christian faith demands effective preaching. Preaching is essential to Christianity. Christianity began with the proclamation of an event … the essence of Christianity is preaching" (Broadus, 1870, 70). The pulpit has throughout history been the primary venue of confrontation. From the Old Testament prophets to Paul's letters, the figure behind pen or podium delivered the gospel message while confronting unholy lifestyles. Today one wonders if preaching has not changed and evolved into a more tamed, predictable practice. Maybe this is due to the church's identity crisis when it comes to Jesus.

Pastors and congregations have created a messiah more to their liking—a Jesus who, though more likeable to the masses, is alien to the Scriptures. Churches and denominations have conformed the Son of God into a placid, soft-spoken figure who tiptoes around the hard sayings. Congregations are taught about a Jesus who used little volume and followers who saw him as polished and polite, guiding his listeners through spiritual truths as if on a school field trip. Leadership and laity seem convinced that Jesus was entertaining rather than enlightening and comforting rather than convicting, that he never showed excitement in his delivery or raised his voice, that he restrained his passions by showing little, if any, emotion.

But is this Scriptural? Have we somehow forgotten the numerous occasions when Jesus confronted his listeners with a tenacity that startled his audience? What about his indignation that stunned his disciples as he cleansed the temple, driving out merchants and flipping tables? Many modern day congregations seldom preach or construe such events from Scripture. Is the church even uncomfortable with the Jesus of Scripture? Have we made up a Jesus more to our liking? Do we believe that our Jesus was nonconfrontational and so his spokesmen should be as well?

In his book, *Essays of Biblical Preaching*, Jay E. Adams states:

> If there is one characteristic that typifies modern preaching, it is its insipid, obsequious approach to speaking to truth. So unlike the early preachers, the reformers, the greatest preachers of all times, many modern, Bible-believing preachers seem afraid to tell it like it is. And yet that modern phrase, "tell it like it is," indicates that people generally appreciate hearing truth for what it is, even when what they hear isn't altogether pleasant ... Boldness, then, was considered a prerequisite for preaching and, when seen, was noted favorably. The same is true today, no less than it was in apostolic times. Boldness is essential for preaching to the heart, and bold preaching makes an impact on those who hear. What is boldness? The Greek word, *parresia*, means "freedom in speaking, openness, willingness to be frank." It is plain speech that is unencumbered by fear. A bold

preacher is one who has no fear of speaking the truth, even when it hurts. Many ministries are hampered today simply because of the fear of men. Will Mrs. Jones take offense if I preach this?" (Adams, 1982, 15–16)

Today, pastors are graded on a Richter scale of laughs and levity. Their once confrontational style has been exchanged for a delivery more like that of a stand-up comic. Entertainment has so permeated the pulpit that it is no wonder that we hear an endless barrage of "I enjoyed it" at the door, a congregational practice that gives any convicting element back to the speaker. Pastors are ranked not on scriptural integrity or theological truths but rather on the capacity to perform. The outcome is that Christianity's most powerful instrument has been tamed. The lion is declawed, harmlessly tucked behind an enclosure of ritual and tradition. And sad to say, this delivery, though questionable, has grown in popularity. Why? It is nonconfrontational, less threatening, more consumer-friendly—a theological tour that meanders in and out of biblical truths without any call to personal ownership and accountability.

James Berkley states, "Preaching without convincing is like cooking a meal that no one eats" (Berkley, 1986, 10). Calvin Miller reminds ministers:

> Still as crass as it sounds, unless the preached word encounters and changes its hearers in some way, artistry and enchantment cannot be made to have mattered much. The sermon must not at last be cute but life-changing. Tragically, today's sermons often appear as tours accompanied by guides who lead their expeditions as if they were on an elementary field trip, escorting their assemblies with an unimposing, quiet manner, slithering through doctrinal structures in such a way that their troops are seldom changed. Occasionally they notice other tour groups led by guides who seem more passionate, more

driven to confront, but these are seen as radical, extreme, not with the times." (Berkley, 1986, 63)

What we lack is preaching that confronts real life. Congregations today can sit under a sermon that, though it may be scriptural, is void of any real conviction. The preacher's role is not to give a history lesson or to regurgitate notes from a seminary class but rather to take spiritual truths and plant them in the lives of his listeners. Robert Webber makes a critical observation in his book, *The Young Evangelicals*:

> It is clear that the younger evangelical wants to turn away from the business models of leadership and return to biblical principles. Ken Blanchard, the author of the *One Minute Manager*, recently told the registrants of a leadership conference that the "popular model of pastor as CEO is brain dead ... This philosophy will only hurt the church in the long run." Leroy Armstrong, pastor of a church in Kentucky, responded that the mega-church movement of the last twenty years has been led by "superstar" pastors who are now "dying out or burned out" without having mobilized lay people for ministry. As a result, the church, which should be an army, "still looks like an audience." (Webber, 2002, 149)

The greatest threat to the church is a weak, nonconfrontational pulpit. Like the wick of a candle, the preacher stands in the very substance to which he has been called to melt. Pastors who once stood tall are now bowed, their stately forms bent and twisted like a wick in hot wax. The flame, which once burned brightly, now flickers. Oh, some may spark and even make noises, but it's just a matter of time until they are extinguished and lie buried in the material they were sent to confront. Many "pulpiteers" have evolved ever so slowly into puppeteers. Their strings stretch across a congregation rather than lift it toward the heavens.

We live in a day when many of today's clergy have succumbed to the pressures of the masses to stoop a little, to give in, to take the abrasive edge off of the message, to make it more palatable to the listener. They edit the content in an attempt to make it safer and softer. The outcome has been a church that is seldom confronted. Members stroll through the dictates of Scripture as if in a cafeteria line, picking and choosing among the various salads, entrees, vegetables, breads, and desserts. They trek down the line, studying each delicacy as if the chef were on trial.

Preachers have forgotten a Savior who said, "I am the living bread that came down from heaven. If anyone eats this bread, he will live forever. This bread is my flesh, which I will give for the life of the world" (John 6:51 NIV). Jesus was emphatic; *there are no other entrees.* Many in his listening audience chose to leave, to vacate the premises rather than endure the teaching, which to them was too difficult and too demanding, the cost too great. Note that Jesus never gave chase to the crowd, nor did he soften his delivery. Instead, he grieved their loss without changing the content. On the contrary, he confronted those who remained. "From this time many of his disciples turned back and no longer followed him. 'You do not want to leave too, do you?' Jesus asked the twelve" (John 6:66–67 NIV).

In his book, *The Integrity Crisis*, Warren Wiersbe speaks of Aaron's failed leadership in the golden calf incident. He states, "Aaron represents those religious leaders who give the people what they want instead of what they need. They are more concerned about pleasing people than about pleasing God. Aaron's cooperation with the carnal crowd probably made him the most popular man in the camp" (Wiersbe, 1988, 91). He goes on to conclude, "Ministry isn't supposed to be entertainment, and a preacher isn't supposed to be a performer" (Wiersbe, 1988, 98).

Let's face it: the pulpit is the front line of the battle for the souls of man, a place where laity is confronted with the Word of God. It is the heartbeat of our commander in chief and his messengers. These souls are to be watchmen that he has strategically placed on the beachhead of the conflict, single voices who dare not falter or stumble in delivery, people who cannot second-guess and drift along in this offensive. Such a voice must be clear and authoritative and, because of the urgency of what he delivers, strong.

Whitefield said, "I love those who thunder out the Word ... The Christian is in deep sleep. Nothing but a loud voice can awaken them out of it." The man of God will find his inflection moving upward, his volume rising as he grasps the magnitude of what he has been called to do. Passion and emotion will grip his body as he pleads for the souls of men and calls the believer to holiness.

Spurgeon commented to his students:

> I know a minister whose shoe latchets I am unworthy to unloose, whose preaching is often little better than sacred miniature painting—I might almost say holy trifling. He is great upon the ten toes of the beast, the four faces of the cherubim, the mystical meaning of badger's skins, and the typical bearings of the staves of the ark, and the windows of Solomon's temple; but the sins of business men, the temptations of the times, the needs of the age, he scarcely ever touches upon. Such preaching reminds me of a lion engaged in mouse hunting ... We must watch the spiritual state of our people, and if we notice that they are falling into a backsliding condition; if we fear that they are likely to be inoculated by any mischievous heresy or perverse imagining; if anything, in fact, in the whole physiological character of the church should strike our mind, we must hasten to prepare a sermon which, by God's grace, may stay the plague." (Spurgeon, 1998, 86)

Note that Spurgeon understood the enemy and his ability to lurk in the shadows, murmuring behind the sacred desk, "Tone it down. Don't get so worked up. You're making a fool of yourself." Congregants, on occasion, will even assist the demonic dialogue with little regard to the cost. Yet pastors must understand that their position is the front line of confrontation, and it is his right handling of the Word that will expose sin and convict the souls of those he addresses. He must not relinquish the battle to "felt needs" and "how-to" sermons.

Perhaps one more illustration will serve to further demonstrate our present crisis. Recently while returning home, I listened to a prominent preacher here in America delivering a sound biblical sermon. Toward the end of the message, he interrupted his delivery with these words: "Now I don't want any of you to leave feeling guilty." Immediately I thought of the multitudes in his congregation as well as his television and radio audience who probably needed a good dose of guilt: men and women flirting with adultery, teenagers toying with drugs, parents neglecting their children, and more.

My thought was, *What is wrong with guilt? Why not allow the Word of God to cut at the heart if needed?* "All scripture is God-breathed and is useful for teaching, rebuking, correcting, and training in righteousness, so that the man of God may be thoroughly equipped for every good work" (2 Timothy 3:16–17 NIV). Why interfere with the scalpel of God's Word because we prefer personal notoriety? Truth may not be comfortable, but in the long run it is never cruel. This popular speaker demonstrated well what has occurred to many in the ministry.

In his book, *It's Our Ship*, Captain D. Michael Abrashoff states, "Throughout known history, messengers of bad news have flinched from delivering it to irascible or self-deluded rulers for fear of losing their lives or at least their jobs in the process. In his tragedy *Antigone*, for example, Sophocles depicts Creon, King of Thebes, becoming so enraged at a bad news messenger that he kills him on the spot. The irony of this Persian Messenger Syndrome, as some call it, is the recipient's illusion that killing the messenger will kill the bad news. Instead, it often kills the recipient, who winds up destroyed by the facts he refused to hear" (Abrashoff, 2008, 58). May neither the fear of our death nor the shrinking of our congregations frighten us into silence.

Marketing the Pulpit

The secularization (marketing) of the church may be the single most contributing factor in the redefining of preaching. Why? Because marketing the pulpit pushes clergy to identify success based on results, and once results become the driving force of a man's ministry, he will be in bondage to performance. Once he is pushed to perform, then he will most likely compromise biblical teachings. There is a growing preoccupation with numbers and methodology, often at the expense of sound theology. This single factor often turns leadership toward reflecting the heart of the *laity* rather than the heart of *God*. David Potter said, "Once marketing becomes dominant, the concern is not with finding an audience to hear the message but rather with finding a message to hold their audience" (Guinness, Os, 1993, 78).

Confrontation is lost when pastors seek to "hold the audience." They are motivated by fear. Who or what do they fear? They fear the congregation and the possibility of the numbers dropping. They struggle to preach a message that attracts more than it convicts. Tragically, fear rather than Scripture now guides their leadership.

Recently I was teaching a class on evangelism to pastors and staff, all of whom were working on a master's level degree. I began the lecture with a single statement: "The biggest hindrance to pastoral leadership in the area of evangelism is fear." By that I meant that most pastors today tend to cower down in their leadership, especially when it comes to the Great Commission. They are pressured by a congregation that desires "homogenous" evangelism, seeking members who look like them. Instead of confronting the prejudices of people, pastors are bullied into compromise, toning down the confrontational nature of the mandate. They forget that every time Jesus said the word *Samaritan*, Jews cringed. However, it did not stop him from saying it just the same.

The danger today is a glamour that has some how evolved around the preacher. Those in the media, conference leaders, and authors who are popular with the masses—all create a level of expectation toward pastors. Congregations who are able to turn on the TV or radio and hear excellent communicators go to their local church and demand the same. If they are not satisfied, then they simply move around until they find someone who can hold their attention. At that point, they are a consumer shopping for someone who will keep them entertained. The outcome is that preachers abandon the prophetic voice and the cry for true repentance.

By its very nature, *repentance* is a confrontational word and a concept that John the Baptist and Jesus both preached throughout Israel. John—the *forerunner*, as some would later call him—stood at the banks of the Jordan River, "preparing the way." The single word *repent* was like cold water in the face of those who stood on the bank. Every man, woman, boy, and girl, regardless of their station in life, was not exempt. Soldier or priest, master or slave—repent! Yet, tragically, what was a mainstay in New Testament times is seldom heard today.

G. Campbell Morgan said, "A man must have a change of mind before he can have a change of nature." *Metanoeo*, the Greek equivalent of *repent*, means "to change one's mind." It seems to imply that man's role is perhaps more than we originally thought. Like the prodigal, he must "come to himself," a cognitive awakening that undoubtedly is spurred on by the voice of the prophet and the word *repent*. Energized by the Holy Spirit, the Word pierces the heart of the hearer, exposing the thoughts and intentions of that control center.

No word has been more neglected by today's church and those who lead her. Why? The average membership is not receptive to such preaching; most see their lives as somewhat conducive to the dictates of Scripture and not in need of such radical inspection. Others, if not most, are insulted by such a word, perhaps because it wields such power and conviction.

CHAPTER 17

Parable for Preachers

IMAGINE YOURSELF AT THE CLOSED door of your church. Behind you are gathered a host of men and women of all ages. They are in a single-file line down the sidewalk and wrapped around the building. You are second in the formation, directly behind a gentleman who for all practical purposes seems to be much like yourself. Curious as to the reason for the occasion, you tap his shoulder in an attempt to strike up a conversation. Instead of addressing you personally, he turns, smiles, and addresses the whole group. You notice that as he speaks to the group, he is clutching a folder. Its edges are frayed and dirty, showing evidence of countless others who at some point must have clung to it as well. His instructions are simple: "I need each of you to make your way as quickly as you can to the pulpit and read aloud the contents of this folder." He pauses, waiting for the murmuring to subside. When it is quiet, he continues, "Above all else, you are not to change anything within the document. Just read it as it is printed." After he delivers the instructions, he explains that he will go first, read it, and then pass it to the next person. "You will wait outside until it is your turn."

In moments, your instructor enters the church to the applause of a packed house and shuts the door behind him. Curious as to why you are here, you motion for quiet while pressing your ear against the wooden barrier. Desperate, you strain to piece the sounds into a scene. Occasionally you hear clapping interrupt the speaker as he moves through the document. Soon, however, the crowd grows quiet and then becomes agitated, annoyed at the lecture. Jeers and cursing begin to tear at the door. The crowd that was jovial earlier is now calling for the reader's death. You listen now as a riot seems to be in the making, and you breathe a prayer, thankful that you are safe on the other side of the enclosure. Soon sounds of someone being beaten filter through.

Worried about the well-being of your predecessor, you turn to the assembly to report what you are hearing, when suddenly the door explodes open and the teacher's bloodied body is tossed out. He stands and waits for the line to reform. Then, without any fanfare, he hands you the document. With a gentle nudge, he whispers in your ear, "Read it just as it is written."

Wow! You take a moment to grasp the weight of what you are about to do. And then you make your way through the foyer, down the aisle, up to the platform, and behind the podium, where to your amazement the crowd has settled and now waits for your address. Opening the folder, you glance at the first page and move into the presentation. The gathering of men, women, and children nod their approval and even applaud at times. You wonder why your predecessor experienced such a violent reception. Soon, however, in the midst of one of these interludes of congregational approval, you see why.

You glance ahead in the document and notice hard statements—the kind that rip at your heart and will most assuredly aggravate your audience. You think, *No wonder the crowd was so angry. I can't say this. If I say this, there is no telling what these people might do.* At this moment, you are tempted to change the material, to adjust the message, to remove some of the abrasive edges and make it softer. You think to yourself, *I can make this a lot easier and more successful if I adjust some of the wording.* However, in the midst of this mental tug-of-war, you remember your predecessor's counsel: "Read it just as it is written." The difficulty of the preacher will forever be the temptation to tone down the message.

CHAPTER 18

The Confrontational Nature of Worship

A. W. Tozer said, "Worship is no longer worship when it reflects the culture around us more than the Christ within us."

Worship is defined as "the act of adoring and praising God, that is, ascribing worth to God as the one who deserves homage and service" (Grenz, Guretzki, and Nordling, 1999, 122). But is worship confrontational? If worship is man's attempt to encounter his Creator, then perhaps it is correct to assume that this encounter would be a confrontation of sorts. If the character and nature of God are confrontational, then wouldn't an encounter with him be confrontational as well?

In a day of strong emphasis on worship, has worship possibly lost this quality? In other words, has today's church evolved into a gathering of pampered children who must be coddled, humored, cheered up, and coaxed into a good mood? Have we swung the pendulum of worship in an attempt to fabricate an excitement that we lack? Can our modern day worship services actually interfere with our Creator getting in our faces and bringing some things to our attention? To put it simply, can worship rob the membership of an encounter with holiness?

Further, is the purpose of worship a meeting with God or a pleasant experience? Could the average church service, whether contemporary or traditional, be denying those who sit in the pew of a chance to see their condition and correct it? (And let me add that this is not an attempt to pose one style over the other in a worship war, because for years the church has been lulled to sleep by tradition and ritual in the way of music.) Whichever worship style we leaders embrace, are we in danger of disregarding the confrontational nature of worship?

In many circles today, worship has become "an experience for me." It has evolved into a form wherein worship leaders and pastors spend the bulk of their time trying to get and maintain the congregation's attention. Ministers find themselves developing a dog-and-pony show in an effort to keep the congregation entertained, because congregations clamor for an experience rather than an encounter. That last statement is critical. The worship leader must fight the urge to create an experience over that of an encounter.

If an *experience* is the goal of leadership, then the tendency will be to focus on mood, warmth, and atmosphere, as if one were setting up a date rather than a marriage. Keep in mind that we tend to behave far differently when dating than we do in marriage. Dating can be a façade, a put-on, a form of hypocrisy—unlike marriage, which is truth in its raw form. Again, if I am concerned that the service be pleasant, then I may in fact get in the way of what God seeks to do in the life of a member. In other words, though God wishes to invade a believer's life with truth and conviction, I as a leader want no part of it because I want the encounter to be pleasant.

Today the pyramid has been flipped into a gathering where those on the platform are performers and those in the pew are the audience—a meeting that ensures that there will be little change in the hearts of the participants. The congregant becomes a consumer, grading the performance. Yes, there is a measure of worship, but the experience for the most part is fractured. Worship is an encounter that results in a change of heart, behavior, attitudes, and so forth. Wayne Grudem states, "During genuine worship, we will often experience an intensification of the sanctifying work of the Holy Spirit, who is at work continually changing us into the likeness of Christ" (Grudem, 1994, 1008). Grudem seems to be saying that Christlikeness—real change—is accelerated by the depth of the worship. True worship measures the speed of sanctification.

Killing the Church

Today, however, we have "worship wars," where congregations base their approval on style alone. The result is that the church loses sight of what defines a successful service or even what is the objective of worship. For instance, "exciting worship" is a caption often used by local congregations to differentiate themselves from those they deem as dead. But think about it: is there such a thing as "dull worship"? In fact, don't those two words linked together sound like an oxymoron or a tongue-tied moron?

There is a danger when churches remove the confrontational nature of worship. Not only will the worship encounter/experience be fractured, but it threatens to splinter the body of believers. Think about it. Churches aggressively advertise multiple worship experiences that run the gamut—traditional, contemporary, or blended—when in reality it divides the body much like Corinth was divided by personalities. "You are still worldly. For since there is jealousy and quarreling among you, are you not worldly? Are you not acting like mere men? For when one says, 'I follow Paul,' and another, 'I follow Apollos,' are you not mere men? What, after all, is Apollos? And what is Paul? Only servants through whom you came to believe—as the Lord assigned to each his task" (1 Corinthians 3:3–5 NIV). In Corinth, it was personalities. Today it is worship style. And regardless of what fractures the membership, the results are the same, further changing congregations into audiences. Once this occurs, we no longer have pews but theater seats devised for comfort.

Speaking of theater seats, I had an insurance representative come into my office and tell be about a church-building nightmare where the pastor challenged each member to purchase a theater seat for $297 plus tax. Though the man admitted that there was a need for space, he struggled with the cost and extravagance. It didn't help matters when I commented that $300 was half the annual salary of a worker in Zimbabwe—and all of this church's expense was just so the congregation could be comfortable. "What should I do?" Todd asked me. My response was, "Buy a folding chair, and schedule an appointment to speak with your pastor. Tell him that you have decided to buy your own seat and would like to send your $297 plus tax to an orphanage in Zimbabwe.

Though that might seem harsh, where does the extravagance and consumerism of the church stop? In this case, we were talking about a massive sum spent on the *gluteus maximus* of individual congregants. In fact, I receive a steady stream of brochures advertising the latest innovations when it comes to seating. In every advertisement there is the stress on comfort. I often wonder what Paul's reaction might be. Regardless of how we may defend the need for comfortable seating, have we become an assembly of spectators, professional listeners who weekly settle into a reclining position and grade the performance rather than glorify the prince?

Churches offer a smorgasbord of services in an attempt to satisfy everyone, when in reality, they are splintering the body. Further, churches compete with each other, bidding for the best vocalists and instrumentalists and the prettiest faces. They market and develop a public presentation that incorporates the latest in electronics, lighting, and media props while disregarding the power of the Holy Spirit. There is a subtle spirit of "who needs the God of Sinai" when we can light up, smoke up, and power up a performance that leaves the average congregation walking out as if they had just watched a sci-fi movie.

Worship void of confrontation is little more than a production. The by-product of such pageantry results in congregations trying to outdo one another in a quest to pack the house. Tragically, a further commodity of this style of worship is a celebrity status given to those who lead the performance. Keep in mind that once the people become an audience, grading the gathering, then those leaders who score high take on a star status. Perhaps the words of Robert Murray are appropriate: "It is not great talent but great likeness to Jesus."

Before you think I am being unfair, let me add that part of the problem is worship leaders and pastors who are grappling with ADD congregations. By that I mean that the average attendee is often stressed and worn-out. His attention span is short and geared to a very narrow window of interaction. When you add to this problem leaders who may be frightened by a worship experience that might be unpleasant, it is little wonder that the congregation is now in control of the platform and the pulpit. The safest thing for the leadership is to develop a "worship identity" that promises an encounter with the Creator without the guilt.

I consider *The Integrity Crisis* by Warren Wiersbe a must for all ministerial students. It speaks of the "integrity of worship" as an event that is "whole or complete" (Wiersbe, 1988, 21). By his definition, he warns the church to be careful lest her worship become fractured, splintered, and even short-circuited. In other words, our wires get crossed. Worship loses its holistic quality, and though we leave feeling good, it doesn't last much longer than Sunday lunch. Again, if our goal is merely to make the membership feel good, then we will not only have done them an injustice; we will have severed the worship event itself.

Let's go back to our television-and-radio preacher's remarks after giving his congregation some strong words. "Now, I don't want you to leave feeling guilty," he said. Maybe it would be good to pose a list of questions to ministerial students. *Is the primary purpose of worship to make the masses happy? Can the sword of the Lord somehow be made dull by worship that steers clear of conviction? Can clergy become so preoccupied with ensuring the congregation's feelings that they forget about their faith—or their filth?* Perhaps there needs to be a warning, regardless of traditional pageantry or celebration. When the confrontational nature of worship is forfeited, the result will eventually be a people who can and will live in habitual disobedience.

Before we leave this subject, I would like to consider this. If worship is primarily a high-energy, experiential event and nothing more, might it overshadow the preaching of the Word? In some churches, worship may require so much time and energy that by the time the Word is being delivered, the congregation is exhausted. This is not a theory but rather an observation.

Recently, I and my family visited a church where the worship service was packed and the congregation was very demonstrative in their participation. Gifted instrumentalists and vocalists filled the first portion of the service with a rich array of sounds and melodies. Yet once the pastor stood to proclaim what I considered to be a strong expository message, the same participants who moments ago had been highly energetic now sat there, lethargic. Their indifference was so noticeable that my teenage son remarked afterward, "Dad, what happened in there?"

Reflecting later on the service, my thought was the same. What *did* happen? Were we in a war between worship and the preaching of the Word? Was the first part of the service overwhelming the second? Were the parts competing, and if so, what chance did a single voice—especially one not well-endowed—have against the pageantry of the former? I even thought about practical issues such as physical stamina. We had stood, sung, and clapped for a solid forty-five minutes, and though the pastor preached an excellent message, I was tired—and his work was that much harder.

I considered a second factor. Had the first part of the service prepared me to receive the Word of God? An audience leaving a live concert and then being ushered into a classroom could be a challenge to the best of lecturers. The bottom line requires that we address a hard question: did the celebrative worship short-circuit the preaching of the Word?

Reflections for Worship Leaders

Reflection #1: Grasping the Element of Fear in Worship

The element of fear is a factor that adds depth to the worship experience. Fear, awe, or reverence—call it what you will—ensures an attitude of respect for what is about to take place and, more importantly, for the one we are about to meet with. My own encounters with prominent figures have always been characterized by a certain element of fear. I remember being on a flight and meeting with Dr. Adrian Rogers, the pastor of Bellevue Baptist Church in Memphis, Tennessee. My family and I were on our way back to the mission field in Cornwall, England, and he was on his way to Romania to speak at a convention. I must admit that at first I was so nervous I could hardly talk, but in time it turned into one of the great memories of my life. We stood up at the exit door of the plane near a pot of coffee made for us by the flight attendant and talked from 10:00 p.m. until 1:30 in the morning.

Killing the Church

Usually when I come into the presence of greatness, I spend the first few minutes stammering, stumbling over my words. For example, if you were to tell me that I could have fifteen minutes with the president of the United States, I'm afraid that most of the time would be spent in awe rather than conversation. My point is that worship leaders must see the confrontational nature of worship.

Reflection #2: Passion and Purity

If the accuser of the brethren is seeking to silence the church, he may be able to do so by manipulating worship—which, I might add, was Lucifer's goal from the beginning. In other words, Satan sought before the creation of man to pull worship away from its primary objective, an encounter with God. Think about it. If the average church member can avoid a meeting with the true and living Christ, then he can quietly continue on in disobedience. Beyond that, if he can celebrate without being confronted, then in some ways the enemy has won a victory. Our enemy is far more threatened by the purity of one's life than he is by the passion of one's worship.

Reflection #3: Are We Thirsty This Morning?

Worship leaders who seek celebration without confrontation will feel as if they're squeezing a slice of lemon into a second glass of tea. Interestingly, we add lots of things to water to flavor it—Kool-Aid, tea, coffee, carbonation, and so on. It's as if the simple composition of water is not satisfying enough, so we dress it up. The truth is that some of us are just not thirsty enough. Is the taste of water unsatisfying to a man dying of thirst? Of course not. In fact, wouldn't a man lost in the desert, if given the choice, choose a glass of water over coffee, Coke, or tea? The Psalmist cried out, "My soul thirsts for thee." Worship leaders may need to ask, "Are the people I stand before thirsty?"

Reflection #4: Who Will Worship?

Let's admit that it's possible that we can have an encounter with God and not even be aware of it. For example, this happened to Jacob in Genesis 28 and to the two disciples on the road to Emmaus; neither knew that they had been in the presence of deity. I remember being in a hotel once where, sad to say, I spent much of the time unaware that a boxing legend, Sugar Ray Leonard, was also in the same place. In fact, the way I eventually discovered the celebrity's presence was by the excitement of those who knew he was there. Fans who followed boxing were able to identify and immediately point out to me a legend. Once this occurred, I—along with the masses who did not keep up with boxing—wrestled for a look, an autograph, and conversation. Worship is the awareness of God's presence, and only those who know him and have walked with him can initiate this discovery.

CHAPTER 19

Confronting Denominations

T O STUDY THE REFORMATION IS to study Martin Luther. Though considered by many to be the primary catalyst of the movement, Luther never thought of himself as such. According to W. Robert Godfrey in his book, *Reformation Sketches*, "Luther comes to Protestant conclusions not so much out of a desire to change or out of a desire to be a revolutionary but out of a desire to get the church to be consistent with her own most basic principles" (Godfrey, 2003, 6). Note that Luther did not intend to be a reformer, yet he exploded on the scene by addressing an ecclesiastical structure that had gravitated from its purpose. Luther did so with tenacity and intestinal fortitude that few could match. His words, "a desire to get the church to be consistent with her own most basic principles," would catapult him into a confrontation. John Calvin went so far as to recognize that "the Christian is called to combat," and sometimes that means within the body.

Today there is an emerging call to purity, a return to a consistency with the teachings of Scripture. However, there must come with this appeal men and women who are willing to confront and turn the church back, believers willing to square off with the injustices and discrepancies in the organizations of which they are members. As A. W. Tozer said, "Denominations can backslide, too" (Tozer, 1990, 65). Why? Because given enough time, the best of agencies will gravitate toward cumbersome structures and bureaucratic bottomless pits that drain the very memberships they were designed to nurture. In time they sap the church of passion and drive, replacing the mission and purpose with a complicated maintenance regimen that serves little if any of the purpose for which it was created.

The outcome is conglomerates that tend to discourage any honest appraisal. Once members begin to assess a structure or the personalities in that structure, they are seen as troublemakers, disloyal, defiant, and unable to get along with others. The truth is, no institution should be above an appraisal. In his work, *Proclaiming Christ in a Postmodern World*, Craig A. Loscalzo reminds preachers, "The pulpit must learn to proclaim Christ while being a loyal critic of institutional religion, whether in its liberal or conservative expressions" (Loscalzo, 2000, 24). David Buttrick comments, "We are witnesses to grace, not to institutional success stories" (Loscalzo, 2000, 24). If confrontation is exercised in the local church, it must be exercised in denominations as well.

There are some who would argue that denominations are autonomous and operate as such. But is that true? How many within the membership are intimidated into silence for fear of being labeled? Clergy learn quickly that any attempt to confront discrepancies within their denomination will be met with opposition. And though the masses may long for confrontation and correction, those who address it will pay a heavy cost. So, rather than addressing concerns, pastors watch as their denominations gather on an annual basis to feed the dinosaur—while in the hallways they complain about the cost and time involved in its upkeep. Frustrations may abound, but few dare voice these publicly for fear of reprisal by the creature itself. As Leonard Ravenhill puts it when speaking of the reformers, "We cherish the last drop of their blood but watch the first drop of our own" (Ravenhill, 1959, 41).

Most members know that the pecking order is well-established and will protect itself if need be. So the problem remains under the surface, because disgruntled members fear the reprisal of the beast. Sad to say, we lack the courage Andrew Murray speaks of in his classic, *A Life of Obedience.*

A story in ancient history illustrates this obedience. A proud king, with a great army following him, demands submission from the king of a small but brave nation. When the ambassadors have delivered their message, the king of the small nation calls on one of his soldiers to inflict on himself a fatal stab wound. He does this at once without a question. A second is called, and he too obeys the unusual command. A third is summoned; he too is obedient to death. Then the king tells the ambassadors, "Go and tell your master that I have three thousand such men. Let him come ahead, if he must." (Murray, 1982, 58)

To address those institutions that we love and are a member of, those peers we hold dear, is one of the toughest things a minister may be called to do. But to ignore the mandate may in the end be seen by God as an act of treason. Let me illustrate at a personal level; though it required no blood, it did convict.

During a finance committee meeting, a question was raised about continuing to support the association of which our church was a member. One of our senior adults asked what purpose the association served in our local area. He was simply verbalizing what the general membership was wondering. In other words, what benefit had this organization been to a church battling to remain in a transitional area. The speaker went on to note that it had been years since any of the association's staff had visited, let alone provided any encouragement.

What was even more interesting was the association's stated purpose: "to encourage, coordinate, and support the churches of our association in the fulfillment of Acts 1:8, the mission mandate of our Lord Jesus Christ." Though the statement sounded good, in my nearly fifteen years at the church I had never had the director visit a worship service, drop by the office, or—if I remember correctly—even call. The director had failed to follow his own statement of purpose.

What made it worse was that I had, in my first few years, visited his office, sent letters inviting him to come, and let him know of the difficulty of our work. But because of the perception that denominations are autonomous, I was reluctant to stick my neck out, not wanting to be blackballed by an entity that—let's face it—could be instrumental in my relocation if I got in trouble. Most pastors are very much aware of these organizational structures and understand that the local church uses them when they seek a new pastor.

The bottom line is this: denominational leaders can affect the hiring process of ministerial leadership. Their power to influence search committees can result in a candidate who, though he is qualified, stands little chance of moving forward. Clergy recognize this subtle factor and therefore avoid healthy and necessary confrontation within the denomination—or worse, they simply don't care. In his book, *Leading Change*, John Kotter states, "By far the greatest mistake people make when trying to change organizations is to plunge ahead without establishing a high enough sense of urgency in fellow managers and employees. This error is fatal because transformation always fails to achieve their objectives when complacency levels are high" (Kotter, 1996, 4).

Denominational Identity:
A Critical Component to Confrontation

A problem today may be the growing nondenominational movement. Historically, denominations evolved as local congregations migrated around certain tenets of the faith, establishing theological and doctrinal boundaries. But today the church is witnessing a loosening of such affiliation. Congregants have come to see denominational "distinctives" as obstacles, nuisances, and barriers keeping out would-be joiners. Today multitudes tear down fences, never bothering to ask why the fence was erected to begin with. G. K. Chesterton warned, "Don't ever take down a fence until you know the reason why it was put up." Denominations, which were once seen as the primary means of accountability, are now tossed aside as relics of the past. The result is that groups are stripped of any doctrinal clarity (theologically or structurally), and their beginnings are often made up of loose, if not nonexistent, belief systems. This is not always the case, and some groups that began as nondenominational soon gravitated toward some form of accountability and affiliation. Added to this are ministers who were never trained in denominational institutions.

What does this have to do with a discussion on confrontation? Belief systems are in and of themselves confrontational by nature. They serve to remind the general populace of the disciplines of the church, and though in evangelical circles those may appear to divide, they in fact are designed to protect the body of Christ. I thank God for Presbyterian, Methodist, Assembly of God, and other denominational groups. Why? Because they ensure that there is some attempt to hold us all accountable to the main components of our faith.

In the beginning, the early churches were quickly tied to the church in Jerusalem as well as to each other. Whether the council at Jerusalem or the circulating letters of the apostles, both were designed to keep the corporate body on the same page. Though denominations may stress different aspects of the faith, they are still joined together by biblical truths—perhaps loosely but united just the same. These truths are by far the first line of defense when one seeks to join a church. You may not like the thought of a revival of denominational identity but it could be paramount to the future integrity of the church.

Some might argue that the present nondenominational movement is an ecumenical movement, but I would say differently. To disregard denominational identity and parameters and allow the flock to run free could undermine the integrity of the church and the Great Commission. Consider again G. K. Chesterton's statement: "Don't ever take a fence down until you know the reason why it was put up" (Wiersbe, 1988, 21). Perhaps we could say it this way: denominational identity is a form of confrontation that in the end helps to define who we are. If we remove it for the sake of unity, then we may commit a grave error.

CHAPTER 20

Warnings Before You Start

Warning 1: Don't Go Half-Cocked

A COURSE OF RESTORATION IS MANDATORY if confrontation is to be biblical. To address defiant, willful, and public disobedience without the hope of returning the person to a viable part of the body is to be in direct violation against the Scripture. "Brothers, if someone is caught in a sin, you who are spiritual should restore him gently. But watch yourself, or you also may be tempted" (Galatians 6:1 NIV). Churches that launch out into a campaign of purging the rolls—or worse, addressing those who are living outside the tenets of the Word of God without any real process of reclamation—may do more damage than if they had chosen to do nothing at all. This is not only a warning for the body at large but also for individual members.

Persons who take it upon themselves to police the rolls, approaching members about half-truths, allegations, and opinions based on pet peeves, will destroy the testimony and witness of an entire congregation. No one should proceed without proper training and guidance from pastoral and lay leadership. Remember that this is to be a church-wide function, a procedure in which the whole body is involved. If the church has taught this to the membership and has incorporated it into new member assimilation, then there should be no misunderstanding as to how and when it is to be exercised. A church that goes off half-cocked, swinging a pistol like Barney Fife and launching out with a vision statement of "nip it in the bud," will short-circuit the Great Commission. Again, there must not be loose cannons or those who work outside the auspices of the church.

Warning 2: Check Your Heart at the Door

There are those in the body who seem to delight in this sort of ministry, relishing the opportunity to "set people straight," and they resemble a preacher who smiles during a sermon about hell. They exhibit a "pre-whale Jonah" kind of heart, and though it may be buried deep, it will come to the surface at the point of confrontation. What frightens these crusaders the most is the possibility of repentance before they have finished their assault. Churches who train their membership in the skills of confrontation will find their most daunting task to be that of reigning in such novelists. Those members must first comprehend that the church is not talking about "pulling up tares" but rather "protecting wheat."

Warning 3: A Confrontational Nightmare

Homosexuality may be the case that will test and even define the future of many churches, especially in the arena of confrontation. Why? With a growing homosexual population, more conservative congregations may deny membership. Once this occurs, the person denied membership could seek legal representation, thereby throwing the church into a publicity nightmare. How?

The individual may seek to prove in a courtroom that the church is exercising a form of discipline in a discriminatory manner. In the average church today, which seldom exercises confrontation or discipline, it will be easy to prove in the case of homosexuality that one is being singled out. Churches that allow, let's say, a person in a live-in, adulterous relationship to continue his church affiliation, while at the same time denying membership to a practicing homosexual, will find themselves in a legal battle. Such churches will quote the authority of Scripture as their guidelines for membership, seeking to enforce it in one area while making an exception in another.

Now, the question is, what can churches do to be Christlike while, at the same time, maintaining the integrity of the church? They must adopt a procedure in which potential members are given private counsel and their memberships are voted on at an alternate time. Every incoming member's lifestyle must be examined in light of the Scriptures. For example, if a new member is living in direct defiance to a command of Scripture, then this must be addressed prior to their being assimilated into the church. If the local church ignores this, the government could eventually force congregations to accept those whose lives are in clear violation of the Scriptures. The only way to combat this is for churches to adopt disciplinary measures that confront habitual, public disobedience in a redemptive way and use these same standards to check all incoming members. For leaders, the road may be rocky. However, only churches that have established clear guidelines will survive the judicial incubus that is sure to come.

A church often faces an awkward task when, in the middle of a public invitation, an individual, a couple, or even a family comes down the aisle and wishes to join the church. Keep in mind that I am not talking about people who are coming for salvation and converting to Christianity but about those who wish to move their memberships from one church to another. Men and women must be denied membership when their lifestyle is one that the church views as contrary to Scripture. If membership acceptance is based on congregational or leadership preference rather than the Scripture, a church will be in trouble. In other words, if the leadership or congregation is lenient on cohabitation while strict on homosexuality, then the church will end up in court.

CONCLUSION

Years ago as a young man, I came within a single decision of destroying my life. In one relationship, the potential for disaster was there. But as Paul might say, thanks be to God that a brief interruption at a critical moment interfered with a compromise that would have changed my life forever. Looking back now, I see that this brief lapse in the events of that evening forced me to return home, where a family photograph would shake me to my senses. In other words, God used a picture to confront me about what I was about to do and the impact that decision would have made on the lives of others. Destinies of countless individuals would have forever been altered had I gone down that road.

Now, decades later as I reflect on the events, I am aware of those around me who loved me, those who saw the signs of a reckless life but did nothing to stop me. Either they loved me too much to intervene or they were too afraid. Regardless, their failure to confront me nearly cost me everything I hold dear. Some might read this and immediately imagine all sorts of criminal acts, and there is little I can do to correct that. But I have never murdered anyone, and I have only slept with one woman, my wife. As to my guilt, Christ knows.

Who should share the blame for this? No one. I and I alone bear full responsibility. This work has not been my attempt to shift the fault but rather to awaken the need in all of us to confront, to get in the faces of those around us and stop them before they wreak havoc in their lives as well as the lives of those they love.

Confrontation is a discipline of the faith that cannot be ignored or pushed to the side. To do so will affect heaven. I beg you to confront, to sound the alarm, to risk relationships for the sake of integrity and holiness. This side of eternity, you may lose a friend, but on the other side you may hear, "Thank you. Had it not been for you, I would have gone down the wrong road."

Mother Theresa said, "We ourselves feel that what we are doing is just a drop in the ocean. But the ocean would be less because of that missing drop" (Bose, Ruma, and Lou Faust, 2011, 51).

ABOUT DR. JEFF PARKER

A pastor, missionary, and former US Army chaplain, Dr. Jeff Parker has spoken in churches and to Christians around the world. His leadership in a variety of settings—from the mission fields of Africa to the churches of England and now to his own country—uniquely qualifies him to speak to the subject of confrontation. Today he pastors an inner-city church in the capital city of Jackson, Mississippi. His commitment to aggressively address the problems of a transitional community have resulted in a wide assortment of programs designed to help the hurting. This mindset is also repeated in mission enterprises in his much-loved second home of Zimbabwe, Africa.

Dr. Parker attended Mississippi State University, where he received his bachelor's degree, followed by New Orleans Theological Seminary, where he received his Master of Divinity. After some years overseas, he returned to Reformed Theological Seminary, where he earned his Doctorate of Ministry. Born in Niagara Falls, New York, he now resides in Brandon, Mississippi, with his wife of thirty-four years. They have four children.

For additional information about speaking engagements, please contact:

Dr. Jeff Parker
jeffparker@ssbaptistchurch.com

Sermon Suggestions

Title: Accountability
Text: Ecclesiastes 4:9–10

I. Why should I be accountable to someone?
    A. Scriptural teaching
        1. Christians are to submit to one another (Ephesians 5:12).
        2. Christians are to bear one another's burdens (Galatians 6:2).
        3. It protects me from Satan and helps build purity of life (2 Timothy 2:22).
        4. I will have to give an account of my entire life to God (Romans 14:12). Therefore, I want to use every means possible to live a godly life.
    B. Practical advantage-accountability works!
        1. Principles from everyday life
            a. Bathroom scales
            b. Tests and grades
            c. Speed limits on highways
        2. The flesh is weak and on our own we tend to give up too easily. If we tell ourselves we will do something, we have only ourselves to answer to. But if we tell someone

else what we are or are not going to do, we double our accountability.

II. Why do some people refuse to have an accountability partner?
   A. Pride
   B. Lack of total commitment
   C. Fear that others will look down on them if they really know them
   D. Laziness: no desire to become disciplined
   E. No knowledge of how to do it

III. What type of person should be my accountability partner?
   A. A growing Christian who is able to challenge you (Proverbs 27:17; 13:20)
   B. One with whom you can be open and honest

IV. What do you do with your accountability partner?
   A. Establish goals together.
   B. Share: strengths and weaknesses, quiet-time insights, answers to prayer, Scripture memory verses, note-taking insights.
   C. Confess to one another and pray for each other consistently (James 5:16, Matthew 18:19).
   D. Encourage and challenge each other (Hebrews 3:13, Romans 15:14).
   E. Check on each other (Acts 15:36).

Additional Sermon Materials on Confrontation

Title: Resolution

Text: 2 Thessalonians 3:6–15

I. Recognition of the problem is a critical first step (v. 11).
   A. Note first that Paul states first his awareness of the problem and how he came about the knowledge in v. 11.
   B. Second, he clarifies the matter of "idleness" and "busybodies" as affecting the church.
   C. Third, Paul speaks to his own work ethic as the proper example to the local church at Thessalonica. Again, the character of the "confronter" is paramount to the process.

II. The biblical admonition is made clear (v.10). There is no hesitation in Paul's counsel: if anyone is not willing to work, then he is not to eat, either.

III. The offense of idleness is considered a biblical discipline. Avoiding idleness is a trait of a true believer and one that both Paul and the others followed.

IV. There is appropriate counsel to the offenders as to how they can correct the problem (v. 12).
A. The action needed: "to work"
B. A proper attitude: "in quiet fashion"
C. The outcome: they are able to "eat their own bread" and not be a burden to others freeing up resources for those in genuine need

V. There is also counsel to fellow members (vv. 6, 14).
A. If anyone does not obey, Paul says to "take note of the offender." This could mean to watch the person in order to ensure that your observation is, in fact, correct. As we have noted, there is danger in confronting someone with insufficient information.
B. "Do not associate": remove the offender from fellowship and separate oneself from the individual. This is to be done by the church as a whole, not by a few, as it would only serve to divide the church.
C. The church has a clear objective: that the one being disciplined will recognize the error of his ways and thereby be shamed into repentance.
D. Paul also warns the believers not to "regard him as an enemy but rather admonish him as a brother." There is always the danger of anger and resentment driving the process rather than the love of Christ.

VI. A secondary warning is given to all involved (v. 13). This bit of counsel was probably a response to a tendency on the part of his audience to dread the confrontation. They may have even developed an attitude of "if you can't beat 'em, join 'em," further undermining the church. Note: Willful, public disobedience will in time affect the whole body, encouraging bad behavior in others.

BIBLIOGRAPHY

Abrashoff, Michael D. *It's our Ship.* New York, Boston: Business Plus, 2008.

Adams, Jay E. *Essays on Biblical Preaching.* Grand Rapids, Mich.: Ministry Resources Library, 1982.

Andrews, Andy. *How Do You Kill 11 Million People?* Nashville, Tenn.: Thomas Nelson, 2011.

Armstrong, John H. *The Compromised Church.* Wheaton, Ill.: Crossway Books, 1998.

Barclay, William. *Letters to the Corinthians.* Philadelphia: Westminister Press, 1954.

Barlow, Lauren. *Inspired By Tozer.* Ventura, Calif.: Regal Books, 2011.

Barna, George. *Think Like Jesus.* Nashville: Integrity Publishers, 2003.

Barnett, Paul. *Focus on the Bible: 1 Corinthians: Holiness and Hope for a Rescued People.* Great Britain: Christian Focus Publications, 2000.

Berkley, James D. *Preaching to Convince.* Carol Stream, Ill.: Word Books Publisher, 1986.

Blaikie, William. *Expository Lectures on the Book of Joshua.* Birmingham, Ala.: Solid Ground Christian Books, 1893.

Blanchard, Ken, and Mark Miller. *Great Leaders Grow.* San Francisco, Calif.: Berrett-Koehler Publishers, Inc., 2012.

Boice, James Montgomery. *The Epistles of John.* Grand Rapids, Mich.: Zondervan Publishing House, 1979.

Bose, Ruma, and Lou Faust. *Mother Teresa, CEO.* San Francisco, Calif.: Berrett-Koehler Publishers, Inc., 2011.

Brinkley, Douglas. *The Notes: Ronald Reagan's Private Collection of Stories and Wisdom.* New York, N.Y.: HarperCollins Publishers, 2011.

Brown, Stephen. *No More Mr. Nice Guy.* Nashville, Camden, N.Y.: Thomas Nelson Publishers, 1986.

Bruce, F. F. *The Epistles of John: Introduction, Exposition, and Notes.* Old Tappan, N.J.: Fleming H. Revell Company, 1970.

Burge, Gary M. *The NIV Application Commentary: Letters of John.* Grand Rapids, Mich.: Zondervan Publishing House, 1996.

Canfield, Jack. *The Success Principles.* New York: Harper, 2005.

Clark, Gordon H. *First Corinthians: A Contemporary Commentary.* Jefferson, Md.: The Trinity Foundation, 1975.

Dungy, Tony. *Uncommon Life: Daily Challenge.* Carol Stream, Ill.: Tyndale House Publishers, Inc., 2011.

Fabry, Chris. *Coming Back Stronger.* Carol Stream, Ill.: Tyndale House Publishers, 2010.

Fagen, Herb. *Duke We're Glad We Knew You.* New York, N.Y.: Citadel Press, 2006.

Fey, Harold E., and Margaret Frakes. *The Christian Century Reader.* New York: Association Press, 1962.

Frost, Michael, and Alan Hirsch. *ReJesus.* Peabody, Mass.: Hendrickson Publishers, Inc., 2009.

Godfrey, Robert W. *Reformation Sketches.* Phillipsburg, N.J.: P & R Publishing, 2003.

Grudem, Wayne. *Systematic Theology.* Grand Rapids, Mich.: Inter-Varsity Press, 1994.

Guinness, Os. *Dining with the Devil.* Grand Rapids, Mich.: Baker Books, 1993.

Gutzke, Manford George. *Plain Talk on Joshua and Judges.* Atlanta, Ga.: The Bible For You, 1988.

Hamlin, John E. *Inheriting the Land: A Commentary on Joshua.* Grand Rapids, Mich.: Wm. B. Eerdman's Publishing Co., 1983.

Hastings, James. *The Speaker's Bible: The Gospel According to St. Luke.* Grand Rapids, Mich.: Baker Books, 1978.

Hiebert, D. Edmond. *James.* Chicago: Moody Press, 1979.

Hybels, Bill. *Courageous Leadership.* Grand Rapids, Mich.: Zondervan, 2002.

Iacooca, Lee, and Catherine Whitney. *Where Have All the Leaders Gone?* New York, London, Toronto, Sydney: Scribe, 2007.

Jeschke, Marlin. "Fixing Church Discipline." *Christianity Today* 49, no. 8 (August, 2005).

King, Larry. *Truth be Told*. New York, N.Y.: Weinstein Books, 2011.

Kotter, John. *Leading Change*. Boston, Mass.: Harvard Business School Press, 1996.

Krauss, Jim. *The Laugh-a-Day Book of Bloopers, Quotes & Good Clean Jokes*. Grand Rapids, Mich.: Revell, 2012.

Larson, Craig Brian, and Drew Zahn. *Perfect Illustrations*. Wheaton, Illinois: Tyndale House Publishers, Inc, 2002.

Larson, Knute. *Holman New Testament Commentary: 1 & 2 Thessalonians, 1 & 2 Timothy, Titus, Philemon*. Nashville, Tenn.: Holman Reference, 2000.

Lewis, Ralph L. *Persuasive Preaching Today*. Ann Arbor, Mich.: Litho Crafters, Inc., 1977.

Lovelace, Richard F. *Dynamics of Spiritual Life*. Downers Grove, Ill.: Inter-Varsity Press, 1979.

Lucado, Max. *In the Grip of Grace*. Dallas: Word Publishing, 1996.

Lyons, Gabe. *The Next Christians*. Colorado Springs, Colo.: Multnomah Books, 2010.

MacArthur, John. *The MacArthur New Testament Commentary: 1 Corinthians*. Chicago: Moody Press, 1984.

MacArthur, John. *The MacArthur New Testament Commentary: Matthew 16–23*. Chicago: Moody Press, 1988.

Mandela, Nelson. *Conversations with Myself*. New York: Farrar, Straus, and Giroux, 2010.

Marshall, Catherine. *Mr. Jones, Meet the Master*. New York: Fleming H. Revell Company, 1949.

May, Steve. *The Story File*. Peabody, Mass.: Hendrickson Publishers, 2000.

Maxwell, John. *The Difference Maker*. Nashville, Dallas, Mexico City, Rio De Janeiro, Beijing: Thomas Nelson, 2006.

McManus, Erwin Raphael. *Chasing Daylight*. Nashville, Tenn.: Nelson Books. 2002.

Middlemann, Udo. *The Market Driven Church*. Wheaton, Ill.: Crossway Books, 2004.

Murray, Andrew. *A Life of Obedience.* Minneapolis, Minn.: Bethany House, 1982.

Myra, Harold, and Marshall Shelley. *The Leadership Secrets of Billy Graham.* Grand Rapids, Mich.: Zondervan, 2005.

Oher, Michael. *I Beat the Odds.* New York: Gotham Books, 2010.

Packer, J. I. *Hot Tub Religion.* Wheaton, Ill.: Tyndale House Publishers, Inc., 1987.

Pennington, Chester. *God Has a Communication Problem.* New York: Hawthorn Books, Inc., 1976.

Pink, Daniel H. *Drive: The Surprising Truth about What Motivates Us.* New York: Riverhead Books, 2009.

Ramsey, Dave. *EntreLeadership.* New York: Howard Books, 2011.

Rath, Tom. *Strengths Finders 2.0.* New York: Gallup Press, 2007.

Ravenhill, Leonard. *Why Revival Tarries.* Minneapolis, Minn.: Bethany House, 1959.

Rees, Paul S. *Don't Sleep Through the Revolution.* Waco, Tex.: Word Books, 1972.

Reynolds, Simon. *Why People Fail.* San Francisco: Jossey-Bass, 2012.

Rice, Condoleezza. *Extraordinary, Ordinary People.* New York: Three Rivers Press, 2010.

Rieger, Tom. *Breaking the Fear Barrier.* New York: Gallup Press, 2011.

Schaffer, Frances A. *No Little People.* Wheaton, Ill.: Crossway Books, 1974.

Smith, F. LaGard. *Fallen Shepherds, Scattered Sheep.* Eugene, Ore.: Harvest House Publishers, 1988.

Spurgeon, C. H. *Lectures to My Students.* Great Britain: Christian Focus Publications, Ltd., 1998.

Swindoll, Charles. *The Tale of the Tardy Ox Cart.* Nashville, Tenn.: Word Publishers, 1998.

Tebow, Tim, and Nathan Whitaker. *Through My Eyes.* New York: HarperCollins Publishers, 2011.

Tozer, A. W. *I Talk Back to the Devil.* Camp Hill, Penn.: Christian Publishers, Inc., 1990.

Thomas, Derek. *Let's Study Galatians.* Carlisle, Penn.: The Banner of Truth Trust, 2004.

Wagner, Peter C. *Effective Body Building*. San Bernardino, Calif.: Here's Life Publishers, Inc., 1982.

Walker, Harold. *Power to Manage Yourself*. New York: Harper & Brothers Publishers, 1955.

Webber, Robert E. *The Younger Evangelicals*. Grand Rapids, Mich.: Baker Books, 2002.

Wiersbe, Warren. *Be Loyal*. Wheaton, Ill.: Victor Books, 1980.

Wiersbe, Warren. *The Integrity Crisis*. Nashville, Tenn.: Oliver Nelson Publishers, 1988.

Wooden, John, and Steve Jamison. *Wooden on Leadership*. Columbus, Ohio.: McGraw-Hill, 2005.